Bone Crack

Other Books By
Bette Golden Lamb & J. J. Lamb

Books in the Gina Mazzio RN Medical Series:
Bone Dry
Sin & Bone
Bone Pit
Bone of Contention
Bone Dust

Other novels by Bette Golden Lamb & J. J. Lamb:
Sisters in Silence
Heir Today...
The Killing Vote

By Bette Golden Lamb:
The Organ Harvesters

By J. J. Lamb (Zachariah Tobias Rolfe III P.I. Series):
A Nickel Jackpot
The Chinese Straight
Losers Take All
No Pat Hands

Bone Crack

By

Bette Golden Lamb
&
J. J. Lamb

TWO BLACK SHEEP PRODUCTIONS
NOVATO, CALIFORNIA

iii

Bone Crack

www.twoblacksheep.us

ISBN-13: 978-0-9851986-7-1
ISBN-10: 0-985198672

Cover Design: Chelsea Erica Lamb
            www.chelsealambcreative.com

Dedication

To Julie Smith, author, editor, publisher, book promoter, and friend, who gave "Gina" new life and saved our collaborative asses.

Acknowledgments

As always, our gratitude, thanks, and love to what has to be the world's greatest critique group —
Margaret Lucke, Shelley Singer, Nicola Trwst &
Judith Yamamoto

Bette Golden Lamb & J. J. Lamb

Prologue

Vlad Folo looked at the woman splayed on the bed. Her legs were spread wide, held down with strips of satin. Her thin arms were tied together high above her head.

No matter how hard he tried, he never could get it right. It never matched his dream.

Daggers of fear screamed from her eyes, but she was voiceless, silenced by a black, spit-shiny rubber ball jammed into her mouth, held there with a strip of gauze wrapped twice around the base of her skull.

Vlad raised his arms and clasped hands, stretched his naked, sweat-soaked body from side to side. He stood at the foot of the bed and looked down at the woman's soft, milky skin; her voluptuous jiggling breasts, and her wiggling hips, all struggling for freedom.

Drops of sweat continued to crawl down his torso; he could feel his cock stir.

But he was in no hurry.

He wanted to feel something other than curiosity, or lust, or that she was only a vessel of relief. He wanted *something* to crawl inside his skin, crawl inside his gut and make it zing. He wanted to cringe with that helpless feeling, as she must, of being totally at someone else's mercy.

He couldn't imagine it.

He tried, felt nothing.

Nothing!

Watching his every move, the woman's eyes widened while his engorgement reached its maximum. Guttural grunts from her throat were the sounds of a trapped animal.

Oh, yes, he was going to fuck her. The only question was: Would he kill her, too?

Bette Golden Lamb & J. J. Lamb

Chapter 1

Tuva jumped onto the sofa and carefully placed one paw at a time onto Gina and Harry's legs, then sprawled across both their laps. She looked up at Gina with big yellow eyes, waiting patiently for a neck scratch.

"Looks like you're finally beginning to trust us, Gina said, leaning over to talk to the cat.

"And it's only taken two years!" Harry smiled, watched Tuva's tail twitch back and forth.

"I'm glad we whisked her away from the shelter." Gina stroked Tuva's grey-and-white-striped fur. Soon the cat sounded like a well-tuned motorboat.

Harry put his head on Gina's shoulder. He turned and kissed her throat, smiled up at her. "I swear this is the happiest I've been in a long time."

"Funny, I thought by now you'd be restless, wanting to hit the road again—hook up to a new travel nurse assignment." She turned and kissed his lips and rubbed her cheek against his. "It's been a whole year."

"I'm enjoying the ICU gig at Ridgewood." He put the cat down on the floor and folded Gina into his arms. "You can't imagine how much I miss this when I'm on the road."

"Careful, next thing I know, you'll let the hospital lull you into becoming a charge nurse." She let out an exaggerated sigh. "Oh, rats, how will I live with you and a swelled head."

He nuzzled her neck again.

Gina ran her fingers through his mop of curly hair and stared into his soft, blue eyes.

It's finally time. The right time.

"I've been giving a lot of thought to the critical question of when we should get married."

3

It took a moment for it to sink in. Harry stiffened, held her at arms' length. "You mean it ... you really mean it?"

She nodded.

"Don't feel pressured," he said. "You know what I want, but you have to be sure." Before she could answer, he pulled her back into his arms. "I mean ... no backing out this time ... please!"

"It's taken a long time, but it's finally sunk into my thick head—my ex-husband is really dead. And every morning for the past month, I've been feeling free. Really free."

Harry was up, headed for the kitchen.

"What are you doing?" She could hear him banging things around, and in a few minutes he returned with a bottle of champagne and two tall flutes. He set them on the coffee table.

"I wondered what that bottle in the back of the fridge was for," she said. "I kept meaning to ask you."

"Well, if you were really paying attention, you'd realize it's been in there for more than a year." He gave her a silly grin. "I kept biting my tongue so I wouldn't say anything ... didn't want to push you, wanted you to know we didn't have to get married ... that I was here for you no matter what."

Harry undid the twisted wire at the top of the bottle, took off the foil, and popped the cork. The noise made them both laugh.

She watched him fill their glasses and said, "Let me toast first." He first looked surprised, then disappointed. "Please!"

"Go for it!"

"To the man who's stood by me, believed in me when no one else did—not even myself." She kissed his hand. "To you."

He lifted his glass. "To my beautiful Gina ... the only one I'll ever love."

* * *

They stumbled back into the apartment after a long dinner celebration. A huge meal at Mario's—their favorite local Italian restaurant. Both were tipsy from the earlier champagne and the red wine they'd downed with a chicken parmigiana/spaghetti dinner. They were also high from the plans they'd tossed back and forth across the table—everything was finally coming together.

Gina flung her sweater across the purple sofa and started dancing around the room. Harry turned on a digital Santana and they danced together for several minutes She plopped down on the couch, her head spinning, her heart racing and watched his hips grind and bump her way. The heat in her groin was making her feel breathless—then the phone rang.

Gina jerked around to scan the receiver's window. "It's ... it's Lolly Stentz!"

"Your friend from the Bronx?" Harry turned down the music.

Gina nodded.

"Well, hi there, stranger," she said into the phone. "It's about time. You've been here for two months and I haven't heard word one from you."

She pressed the phone closer to her ear. "What? I can barely hear you. Talk louder." Gina pressed the speaker button so Harry could listen in on the conversation.

Lolly's harsh whisper raised goose bumps.

"I think someone is about to be murdered."

Bette Golden Lamb & J. J. Lamb

Chapter 2

Gina moved quickly through a crew of construction workers near the new, almost-completed Cardio-Surgical wing. Once finished, the new addition would be a totally independent unit within Ridgewood Hospital. It was exciting.

She knew the hospital pretty well after four years—it was the first place she worked after her move from New York to California. She'd started in Oncology as a full-time staff nurse, and worked in a number of other departments after that. She'd had her ups and downs, but overall, she liked Ridgewood. The large facility offered a lot of nursing opportunities and room for personal growth that some smaller institutions couldn't match.

For most of the four years she'd been away from New York, she'd lived in fear of Dominick coming to kill her, possibly Harry, too. He couldn't hurt them anymore. She was a free woman.

Gina had even toyed with the notion of moving back to New York. She hadn't mentioned it to Harry, and had no idea how he would feel about it.

She'd been so homesick when she first came to the San Francisco Bay Area, but things had changed and she now realized that moving back to the Big Apple was no longer a real consideration. She had blossomed into a diehard Californian—a truly successful transplant from the East Coast.

Many of the construction men who were building the new CCU connecting hallway recognized Gina. They waved at her—some even gave a respectful hello. There were none of those eye-popping leers; these men had a much better attitude toward nurses than the gorillas she'd had to plow through when she was working in the Bronx.

The in-progress hallway was lit with spotlights, even in the daytime. They tended to blind you more than help you to see.

7

Sometimes when she worked late and the construction people were gone for the day, the empty hallway felt creepy. It reminded her of the dark alleys she'd been forced to walk through when she was a kid. Even after all this time, she still had terrible memories of being beaten and almost raped. She couldn't purge those horrors from her mind—nightmares still forced her into dangerous landscapes where she was running from someone or something.

Thinking about it now gave her the chills.

The big plus about her childhood was her brother, Vinnie. She loved the jerk and was so happy he was not only finished with the military, but was slowly recovering from PTSD. It was good to have him right here in San Francisco and working as a nurse tech in Ridgewood. Not only that, he'd fallen in love with her best friend, Helen. It felt almost incestuous.

The Bronx also made her think about Lolly Stentz and her weird call last night. Lolly had insisted on meeting here in person—didn't want to use email or the telephone. She'd suggested lunchtime, around 12:30.

"I'm new on the unit," Gina had said. "I can try, though. The cafeteria?"

Dead silence.

"Lolly! What's going on? What makes you think someone is going to be murdered?"

"If you can't make the lunch thing, call me. Please! I'll meet with you anytime, anywhere."

As she thought about their brief talk, an eye started twitching—never a good sign.

One thing was obvious: her childhood friend, Dolly Lolly, was truly spooked.

* * *

Gina reached the Coronary Care Unit, which had grown into a small independent medical city for heart disease patients. The docs were now doing surgery in their own separate OR.

She had transferred out of Internal Medicine and was now working in CCU, but her eventual slot was to scrub in for procedures in the Cath Lab. She was looking forward to it.

The Cardio Room had all the latest equipment, which meant a lot of up-to-the-minute technology. It was like being in a space ship—without being weightless.

Everything was compact, from viewing monitors to digital X-Rays. But what really captured her attention was a ceiling-mounted Image Intensifier, with a no-squinting-your-eyes flat viewing screen.

Pretty darn impressive.

She tried to visualize the room the way a patient would. Seeing the arteries and chambers of your own heart up on the wall had the potential to freak-out any person. Gina didn't know how she would feel about it if she were lying on the table. Probably try to pretend her throbbing heart belonged to someone else.

And, with a little bit of Versed and Fentanyl juice mixed into your IV, she probably wouldn't give a damn.

Chapter 3

Gina hurried through the cafeteria line. She could see Lolly Stentz sitting at a table near one of the windows of the crowded cafeteria. It was obvious she was lost in her own thoughts.

Lolly jumped up the moment Gina set her tray down and crushed her in a tight bear hug. Her friend was trembling and she kept hanging on every time Gina started to pull away.

"Hey, hey, girl, what's going on?"

"Oh, Gina, I'm so happy to see you." Lolly finally held her at arm's length and a gush of tears rolled down her face.

Gina yanked a tissue from her pocket and dabbed at the face of one of the prettiest women she knew—Lolly was the kind of woman most men have fantasies about. Her natural blonde hair was almost white and her eyes were such a startling light blue, it was hard to look away.

They finally sat down.

Lolly hadn't gone through the food line—there was nothing in front of her other than an almost empty glass of water. It made Gina feel gluttonous with her tray piled high with red pepper soup, French bread, and a chicken taco. "How about sharing my food. I bought way too much."

"Gina, I can't eat. I've hardly had a bite in the last two days."

"So tell me, what's going on?"

Lolly looked around, leaned over the table and repeated *sotto voce* what she'd said the night before, "Someone's going to be murdered."

Gina could see terror in her eyes.

"Why do you say that? What's going on?"

Lolly took her hand and squeezed it. "Please, Gina, lower your voice. I'm really scared."

11

Old fears clutched at her chest. Gina stared at her food and then pushed her tray away. "You've only been here two months and already someone's trying to kill you? This is San Francisco, not the Bronx ... cool it!"

Gina's smart-ass remark went nowhere.

Lolly started crying again. "You don't believe me, do you?"

"I'm sorry," Gina said. "Of course I believe you. Me, of all people, should know better. I'm one of the most suspicious women on the planet. But you've nailed a job at one of the biggest and most successful cardiology practices in the Bay Area—how bad can it be?"

"I know I should be ecstatic. And you were the one who helped me get my foot in the door. I really appreciated your talking to Bob Cantor on my behalf."

"He's a great physician, easy to know and to work with. I thought you and he would be a match made in heaven." Gina couldn't stop herself—she reached out for a chunk of French bread, tore off a piece, dipped it in the soup, and started chomping on it.

"It's not Cantor or Jon Brichett, but I'm working with their third partner," Lolly said.

"Mort Tallent is the problem?"

Lolly looked around and whispered, "I'm telling you, someone is going to die."

"What makes you think so?"

"It's his books."

"His books? What books?"

"His accounting books ... financial records." Lolly took a deep breath, leaned across the table, and whispered into Gina's ear, "He's committing fraud, Gina. Big time malpractice."

Lolly's voice was so low Gina almost didn't get what she said. When it sank in, she was incredulous.

"How did you get into his books?" Gina said. "Between surgeries, consults, and long office hours, the man must barely have time to breathe. What made you even check into his books? You're his nurse, not his bookkeeper."

They were so engrossed they didn't notice Harry arrive. They both jumped when he sat his tray down with a clump.

Harry leaned over and gave Gina a kiss on the cheek, looked up, and said, "Hi, Lolly. Or should I say, 'Hello, Dolly Lolly?'"

Neither one responded to the teasing.

"Oops! Sensitive about your old name? Hey, you want me to leave? I mean, you seem to be pretty tight into something" He shrugged. "No problem."

"No, no, Harry, stay. It's just that there's not much to joke about today," Gina reached out and squeezed her friend's hand. She could tell Lolly wasn't too keen on Harry being there.

"Start from the beginning," Gina said. She moved her tray closer and took a spoonful of soup, which was now cold. She passed the chicken taco over to Lolly, along with a fork. Lolly pushed it back and shook her head. Her face had blanched to the color of the sour cream in the little cup at the side of the taco.

"It all looked so hopeful," Lolly said. "I thought I'd be working with Bob Cantor. He's a really great doctor; he loves working with patients and he was the one who began showing me the ropes. But I was never going to work with him. After orientation, I became Tallent's nurse."

"It still sounds like a job made in heaven," Gina said.

"Yes! I love the job. I'm not only counseling cardiac patients, I've started doing their stress tests, along with giving IV sedation."

"Weren't you supposed to work your way into assisting with cardio procedures?" Gina said.

"Well, that's up next for me. I'm just easing into it." She reached over and took a bite of Gina's taco. "I've just started placing sheaths into the femoral artery. That's a little scary." She chewed the food slowly. "I'm not used to hanging that far out there."

"Lolly, you can do anything."

"I know I can do it. It's just a little unnerving."

"So you use lidocaine," Harry said. "That should numb the entry point and not hurt the patients too much."

Gina was at the bottom of her soup bowl and sopping up the last drops with the French bread. Talking about the job and the medical procedure seemed to calm Lolly. Color was coming back into her cheeks.

"It is fascinating," Harry said. "Once the sheath is placed, the catheter is passed through and it's not supposed to be painful at all. Really incredible. Blows my mind. That catheter allows them to see all the vascular structures, the heart, the whole circulatory system. I wouldn't mind working with that. I'm really into all that technical stuff."

"Yeah, but there's so much that can go wrong," Lolly said.

"All right, you two," Gina said, her voice very low. "We can talk shop later when we're not on a lunch break. Right now, I want to know why you think Mort Tallent is a murderer

Chapter 4

Morton Tallent sat at his desk sipping a second Mocha Grande. He was trying to work up the energy to see his first afternoon patient. He looked out through the panoramic window of his penthouse office, but instead of enjoying the spectacular view of San Francisco, all he saw was the dreary rain that had descended on the city.

Trying to put off the inevitable, he stalled by glancing at the framed degrees and certifications hanging on a wall. They should have made him proud.

He'd invested fourteen years to create a foundation for his career, which allowed him to sink in another fifteen years creating a practice and building a reputation. He'd accomplished a lot, from Pre-med to his Cardiology Fellowship, but now all he saw was his life slipping away. When he looked at the wall of certificates, all he saw was the documentation for as lost life.

Yes, he'd built a huge fortune over an extended period of time. But his head and heart told him he should have been climbing mountains, sailing the seas, exploring ancient ruins, surfing around the world—being the spoiled scamp of wealthy parents. Now those years were gone and he was locked up in a cell filled with academia and medicine that his parents had forced him into.

Every day he examined sick, tired, people, most of them ill-tempered and unappreciative. Many were waiting for him to make some kind of small mistake so they could sue his ass off. Of course, none of them wanted him to screw up too badly or they wouldn't live to enjoy the lawsuit money they hoped would come rolling in.

He finally pulled up the records for his 2:00 p.m. patient. The computer screen filled with her personal history, past treatments, meds, diagnoses—all emailed to him by the referring internist.

Mort had been getting referral after referral from this particular doctor, who was getting ready to retire and apparently not investing much time doing what he was supposed to do— like heal. This new patient, Katherine Parker, had now been palmed off on Tallent and as the internist had demonstrated previously, he would have no further interest in her.

The coffee was energizing him and as he studied the patient's record, he realized she represented a good candidate for his practice. He turned back to the file again. Yes, she definitely was a good candidate for his outpatient Cath Lab.

He stretched his arms over his head and allowed his attention to slip away from Kathryn Parker's medical records. He hadn't had enough sleep the previous night, which had nothing to do with putting in long hours taking care of patients. Rather, he'd spent the late afternoon and evening at his upscale health club, where he had taken a long swim, an even longer steam, and then kept his appointment for an extended massage with Vlad Folo.

Before Tallent left the club, he'd given the Russian another of his special assignments: twenty-five thousand dollars up front, another twenty-five thousand upon completion.

Thinking of Vlad, the cardiologist opened the desk's top drawer, pulled out his cell and stared at the window, with its entire list of new messages.

He felt his heart skip a beat, then another. Vlad had called three times. The last message sent chills climbing up Tallent's back.

Tallent cursed the day he'd met the man.

* * *

Tallent's wife, Annie, had divorced him and moved in with a physical therapist she'd met at a Ridgewood Hospital Christmas party more than a year ago.

16

That innocent meeting was the beginning of Tallent being taken to the cleaners with monthly high five figure alimony payments. He'd agreed to the sum, but it was like a knife ripping through his chest every month when he saw the automatic withdrawal from his bank account.

He met Vlad one day when he'd escaped to the health club in an effort to shut down his brain and simmer down.

The steam room, followed by a trio of single malt Scotch, neither mellowed him nor dampened the anger generated by the betrayal of his wife, the bitter divorce, and the excessive alimony settlement.

The private alcove, with soft music and pastel lotus blossom wallpaper, did nothing to soothe him. He remained a metal coil, compressed and ready to spring open. Vlad Folo, a new body specialist who was very tall, with muscles that popped from every part of his body, probed deeply into Tallent's tight muscles. Soon Tallent was belching out his anger. Vlad's strong fingers stopped in the midst of one of Tallent's tirades about his wife.

"That filthy whore." His Russian accent was at its strongest.

Tallent raised his head and gave Vlad a grim smile.

"Yes! She's a cheating, filthy whore!"

Vlad turned Mort onto his back, started working on his arms, pushing at his tense muscles, probing deep into his chest.

"Do you want me to take care of her?" Vlad's eyes were black daggers.

* * *

Kat Parker was a little early for her appointment with Dr. Morton Tallent. She paced back and forth in the trendy waiting room rather than take a seat in one of the soft, pliable leather chairs that were scattered around the room.

She stopped in front of a large oil painting of a girl sitting in a chair, staring out at the viewer. Kat liked the warm colors and questioning eyes that seemed to say, "What's next?"

17

It was exactly how Kat felt.

Fourteen months ago her husband walked out, left her for a younger, skinnier rendition of what she once was. The men she'd dated since then were mostly from the tech company where she worked. They never seemed to hang around very long after she let it be known she was looking for something more than a fuck partner.

That wasn't enough for her. Period!

She'd tried to get into all the upbeat happiness around her, but mostly she worked with younger people whose lifestyle interests weren't anything like hers. Most of her friends—people she'd known for years as a couple—faded away. She was left at loose ends, flapping in the wind, not able to tie all the strings together.

Kat went back to pacing the length of the waiting room, but she could see she was driving the receptionist crazy. She sat down, grabbed one of the out-of-date fashion magazines on a side table, and flipped through the pages. It was filled with emaciated models wearing clothes she wouldn't be caught dead in, even if she could find one that fit.

One photo featured a woman in an off-blue satiny dress, with a huge waist sash that ended in a massive bow set smack in front at belly button level.

Kat laughed at a mental image of her own belly fighting with that bow, trying to tame it to stay in place. She knew her fat rolls would be pushing it every which way. The model in the picture was probably less than one-half of Kat's fifty three. Little girl bows didn't work for her. She slapped the pages closed and tossed the magazine back on the table—it missed and fell to the floor.

"Ms. Parker, the doctor will see you now."

Kat's heart pounded, her steps were uneven as she followed the receptionist, who could have just stepped out of the magazine she'd been leafing through. They walked down a long, plush-carpeted hallway, bypassing a half-dozen closed doors. Then the receptionist stopped and knocked lightly on a door marked with scrolled, gold letters: Morton Tallent, MD.

"Come in!" took them through the door. "Dr. Tallent, this is Ms. Katherine Parker. Ms. Parker, Dr. Tallent."

The tall, dark-haired, fiftyish man walked around the desk and took her hand—held onto it for a moment. "It's a pleasure to meet you, Kathryn."

"Please call me Kat."

"Have a seat ... Kat." He pointed to two side-by-side, cordovan leather chairs that faced a double-wide, polished wood desk that appeared to hold nothing more than a gleam.

"So, Kat, that must be interesting work—Director of Human Resources for Golden Eye Tech."

"It's challenging to pull together a hodge-podge of different personnel services in a new tech company." She shifted in the seat, trying to get comfortable. "But it's an interesting job. What I'm mostly occupied with these days is trying to find housing for new employees moving in from other parts of the country. It's as if everyone is descending on San Francisco."

He nodded. "I've had a chance to review your medical records, Kat. It looks like your internist has already put you through an extensive panel of tests: Blood work, ECG, echocardiography, stress tests. Everything was relatively normal."

"I know. But I'm sick and tired of having this neck pain. It's been going on forever, yet every test I take turns out negative."

"Your internist has counseled you on lifestyle changes, I assume." He took her hand again and gently squeezed it. "Losing twenty pounds could change some of the minor blood abnormalities you have. Exercise, maybe some therapy or yoga. They could make all the difference."

Kat burst out into tears. "Please, please, stop! I've heard it all before. I know I'm fat, need to lose weight." She grabbed at the tissue he handed her and daubed her eyes and cheeks. "You think I don't know all of that?"

"Well, let's see: We could go ahead and line you up for our Cath Lab and see if there's anything at all that's causing your symptoms."

Love for this man washed over her whole body. It was like the weight of the world had been lifted from her shoulders.

Someone was finally going to help her. Maybe she could really have a life again.

Chapter 5

Lolly was even more jumpy since her get-together with Gina and her fiancé. She and Gina had gone through nurses' training at the same time and afterwards worked together at Jacoby Hospital in the Bronx. Lolly knew how her Italian friend felt about protecting her patients. She had seen Gina defy doctors who treated a patient poorly—she could be fearless, even reckless.

Lolly was one of the nurses on duty in the ER when Gina was admitted, half dead after her husband beat her up and repeatedly jammed a beer bottle into her vagina. Gina was bleeding out when the EMTs brought her to the hospital. The ER staff thought they'd lost her before they could even get her up to surgery. It was a miracle she survived.

Poor Gina! She'd been to the wars and back.

Lolly also liked Harry. Aside from being cute, with a curly mop of hair and kind, blue eyes, she'd heard he was a darn good nurse. She was surprised to see him again in the hospital cafeteria because he usually took out-of-town assignments as a travel nurse. Maybe he was working at Ridgewood because he and Gina were planning to get married soon. The two of them looked very happy together.

She wished the bookkeeper for Tallent, Brichett, & Cantor hadn't confided in her about her suspicions. If what Maria Benke said was true, Mort Tallent was scamming his patients and the government for procedures that may never have been performed.

Lolly really liked this job, had fallen in love with the spaciousness of the penthouse offices where they had their own small surgical unit, along with a four-bed CCU. It was like being in your own medical world without all the hospital

21

bullshit—mainly administrative interference. It had promised to be an interesting place to work until Maria had confided in her.

And that wasn't all of it.

Maria was afraid Tallent was putting people's lives in danger, solely to make money. She said she'd found evidence that many patients hadn't needed the surgeries they'd undergone.

That went beyond scamming—it would make Tallent a dangerous man. And if what the bookkeeper said was true, it would make Lolly a part of his medical malpractice.

Lolly didn't buy it. How would a bookkeeper know what a patient needed for treatment?

But no matter how hard Lolly tried, she couldn't stop visualizing one of the possible side effects of the procedure— blood clots on the loose, lodging in a patient's lungs or brain. No one should have to risk that if they didn't have to.

That kind of practice didn't align with Lolly's career nursing goals and she didn't know what to do with the kind of information Maria gave her.

* * *

Lolly realized that she should have never agreed to go out to dinner with Maria in the first place. Maybe she wouldn't have heard about any of it.

But, there it was: after a few glasses of wine, the bookkeeper started talking about the bundles of money Tallent was raking in from Cardiac Catheterization. "These days, that's just about all he does."

"Couldn't that be an in-house agreement between him and the other docs?" Lolly said. "A lot of docs specialize in different aspects of a treatment."

"Maybe," Maria said. "But I heard him and Dr. Cantor getting into it one evening when they thought the office was empty. And it wasn't just a conversation—they were shouting at each other."

"About what?"

"What else?" Maria said. "Money! Cantor didn't like the way Tallent was raking in the money, or how he was running his practice. Thought he was being unethical by overcharging Medicare."

"Seems to me there's plenty of cash to be made in cardiology without doing any of the things you're talking about."

Maria kept downing more and more wine. The more she drank, the looser her tongue got. "Dr. Tallent really changed after his wife divorced him. He became bitter and angry. Since then, he's been really hard to work with."

"In what way?" Lolly asked.

"He's started accusing me of being too noisy, asking too many questions." Maria had been pretty emotional at that point. "You can't help but be nosy when you're a bookkeeper. It's part of my job to ask the hard questions."

"I think you're worrying too much, Maria."

"It got even worse when his wife was murdered."

"Murdered? Are you kidding me? I thought you said they got divorced."

"This was afterward. Some creep tied her up, did horrible things to her—I can't even describe it, other than she was slit open from neck on down to her ... privates." Maria tossed down the rest of her wine. "It was gruesome."

"When did that happen?"

"About a year ago."

"How did Tallent take it?" Lolly asked.

"Well, it was no picnic. The police came around and questioned everyone, but especially Dr. Tallent. I guess they thought he might have killed her—they'd gone through a pretty bitter divorce." Maria pushed a fork around the plate; she hadn't eaten one strand of her linguini.

"After the hullabaloo died down, nothing changed. He was just as nasty, maybe a little bit worse."

Maria pulled the napkin from her lap and slammed it down on her plate. "I know he's going to kill me."

"What?" Lolly quickly looked around the restaurant to see if anyone had reacted to Maria's outburst. "You can't be serious."

"It's my fault. I just couldn't leave it alone. When I questioned him again about his practice, he warned me to stay out of his business—or else."

Maria's face turned snow white. "I said, 'Or else what?'" Her hands started shaking.

"What did he say?"

"He asked how my mother was doing."

* * *

Robert Cantor had the first scheduled cath. The admitting nurse, Dara, was with the patient in the pre-op holding room. A second patient was scheduled to follow.

Lolly looked at her watch. Dara had probably already given the patient pre-op meds for anxiety while Lolly was checking the viewing monitors with the X-Ray tech. Lolly gave the sterile field and all of the equipment a final once-over.

Preparing for surgery always gave Lolly the chills. In a short time they would have a human being on the table, ready to endure an invasive journey through their circulatory system. The set-up looked fairly benign, but a lot could happen, depending on what they found when that catheter traveled through the coronary arteries.

Lolly tried to calm herself, but she couldn't stop thinking about Maria and what she'd told her. Why hadn't she come to work today?

* * *

Maria Benke looked at the street through the slats of the living room venetian blinds. She sensed that someone was watching her, but she couldn't see anyone outside. She'd been afraid to go to work after her last conversation with Dr. Tallent and had stayed home all day.

24

"Maria!" Her mother's voice traveled down the hallway.

"Yes, Mom. I'm coming. Just a minute." She kept the lights out and looked outside one more time.

Nothing.

Maria stood at her mother's bedroom doorway. "You said my name perfectly. Did you hear that? I think we'll be throwing one heck of party for your seventy-fifth birthday."

"Ish better."

"Let me help you up; you can keep me company while I make us dinner."

Her mother shook her head. "Ooo ired."

"Okay. I'll make a tray for the both of us and we'll watch TV right here. How does that sound?"

Her mother smiled back at her. After six months, she still had a long road ahead of her to recovery from her stroke, but she was a spunky woman. If anyone could do it, she could.

Maria went into the kitchen, poured herself a glass of red wine, and began preparing dinner.

Chapter 6

Vinnie and Helen sat around the dining room table at Gina and Harry's apartment. An almost empty bowl of chicken Caesar salad, a basket of garlic bread, and a bottle of red wine sat in the middle of the table.

Gina looked across at her brother and smiled at his beaming face. He kept looking at her best friend, Helen, with an I-love-you expression—he could barely take his eyes off her. He turned to Gina and dropped a bomb.

"Helen and I have decided to get married."

It took a moment for the words to sink in.

"Wahoo!" Gina and Harry yelled in unison. They jumped up and rushed around the table to give Vinnie and Helen hugs and kisses.

"When did you decide?" Harry said. "Not that it's a big surprise."

"Right before we left the apartment." Vinnie laughed and speared another piece of bread from the basket and stuffed it into his mouth.

"Helen, you're not saying a word," Gina said. "That's usually not a problem for you. Maybe I should be grateful."

"I'm too stunned to speak." Helen really did sound sawed. "He even did the get-down-on-your-knee thing."

"My brother?"

"Oh, go on with you, you little devil," Helen said. "No wonder you and your brother are always tussling."

After a long discussion about how maybe the four of them could get married at the same time, they dug back into the food. Gina was ravenous. When she finally came up for air, she said, "What do the two of you think of Morton Tallent."

"I've taken care of his patients," Vinnie said, "but I haven't had much to do with him other than the usual 'Good morning, doctor' stuff."

"Well, I don't like the guy," Helen said. "He's a phony. He'll talk to his patient's all sweetness and light, and then walk out of the room and give the nurses a bad time."

"What kind of bad time?" Harry said.

"You know, you're-just-a-nurse-and-you-don't-know-shit kind of thing."

"He's never been that way around me in CCU," Harry said. "He's not a warm, slap-on-the-back kind of guy, but I thought he was all right."

"Yeah, but you're a man," Gina said. "I'll bet he treats you a lot differently. I'm with Helen. I've worked with him in CCU and there's no doubt he's a condescending ass."

"Now his partners in crime, Bob Cantor and Jon Brichett, are really great," Helen said.

"I like them, too," Gina said. "I spoke to Cantor about Lolly. That's how she wiggled her way into the job."

"Is that Lolly Stentz? Our Lolly from the home turf?" Vinnie said. "Why haven't you told me she was in town?"

"Truthfully, I haven't seen much of her since she arrived," Gina said. "She literally blew into town and needed a job right away, and off she went. That was only two months ago. I've only seen her once since she started working."

"What's she doing out here?" Vinnie laughed. "I mean, I could have sworn she was a die-hard New Yorker."

"She had her reasons, but it seems Tallent hired her for his office OR and Recovery Unit. Now there's some kind of problem." Gina emptied the rest of the spaghetti onto her plate and took another piece of garlic bread. "Lolly thinks he's doing something unethical."

"Wait a minute!" Helen said. "Isn't Tallent the one whose wife was murdered about a year ago?"

"Yeah," Harry said. "I vaguely remember the gossip about that. Wasn't she screwing around with one of the PTs?"

"Shoot, even I remember some talk about that," Vinnie said.

"I told Gina not to get involved. Let Lolly iron out her own problems." Harry did an all-around refill of the red wine. "But I can tell from the look in her eye, she's not listening to me."

Gina gave him *the look* and said, "She's my friend. I can't ignore *anyone* as scared as she is, much less a friend."

Vinnie suddenly had that frightened fixed stare. "Stay out of it, Gina!" Vinnie said. "I can't take a chance of losing you again. You hear me? Stay out of it!"

Harry jumped up, gently took Vinnie's arm, and walked him off into the living room.

Gina felt her heart clawing at her chest. "I'm sorry, Helen. I thought Vinnie's PTSD was so much better. She lifted her wine glass with a shaking hand and took a small sip. "I should have known better than to say anything."

"He's so improved even I forget," Helen said. "But he still has nightmares, even though it's rare now. She reached across the table and took Gina's hand. "He's very protective when it comes to you." Helen chuckled. "You'd think you were the younger one, rather than it being the other way around."

"Maybe I should go in and talk to him," Gina said.

"He'll be fine. Harry's the best medicine in the world for Vinnie." Helen looked at Gina with a worried face. "But really, I hope you're not planning to get into this situation with your friend Lolly Stentz."

Gina turned away and softly said, "I just don't know.

Chapter 7

Vlad Folo's eyes snapped open.

He held very still, sniffed the air. There was only the smell of the female next to him—that and the rank smell of his own sweat.

When he was sure he could sense no movement in his studio apartment, he allowed his head to move from side-to-side.

Yes, he'd awakened with a jolt from the same dream—the one where he's hiding in his parents' closet, looking through the thin slats at his naked mother bound to the bed—arms tied to the headboard, feet spread and lashed to the bed frame, mouth gagged and silenced. He could hear her grunts as she tried to suck in air.

Mamoushka!

Two men stood over her arguing about who was going first.

Twelve-year-old Vlad knew what they were talking about even before the taller man opened his fly and let his cock spring out of his pants.

Vlad's eyes shifted to his father, who sat in a chair, arms tied behind his back, shouting, "You devils, you'll rot in hell!"

The tall man hovered over his mother, laughing. "Maybe so, traitor, but you'll already be there keeping everything nice and warm for me. Did you think running away would end it, would allow you to cheat our people? Did you really think you'd get away? You can't be that stupid to think that we were finished with you just because you ran away to America?"

"Bastard!"

The other man walked up to his father and punched him in the face. "Shut up or I'll cut out your tongue."

His mother shifted her hips, trying to get away as the man jumped on the bed and mounted her, squeezed her hard with his

31

thighs. He grabbed her ass with both hands and pulled up until she was lifted enough so he could plunge himself inside of her. He rammed her, over and over, faster and harder, clutching her shoulders while the slap of his body against hers tore through the air.

Vlad covered his mouth to keep from screaming.

No, *Mamoushka*. No!

The man soon let out a cry and collapsed. He lay there like a rag doll until the other man yanked at his arm, half pulling him off, then took his place. The other man's pants was already opened and lowered. He jammed himself inside of her, too, his bottom pumped while he yelled, "Bitch, bitch, bitch!"

His father screamed, *"Yóp tvayú mát"*

The tall man zipped up his pants and in an easy stride, walked up to his father, pulled out a knife, and carved a straight line from his father's mouth, down his chin, and onto his chest—his screams were silenced when the man jammed a balled up handkerchief in his mouth. But the air still vibrated with, "Bitch, bitch, bitch!"

"Did you think you were safe from your friends in Minsk?"

Go away. Go away.

Vlad swallowed hard, held his breath to keep from screaming.

It seemed like only a few minutes since his father pushed him into the closet and said, "If they know you're here, they will kill you." He'd kissed Vlad. "I'm sorry, but you will be on your own from now on, and you must hide to survive. They will never stop looking for you."

His father's face was turned to Vlad with eyes that burned through the closet slats into his. The tall man slit his father's throat—blood sprayed everywhere.

Without a word, the man made a sweeping turn to the bed and slashed across his mother's throat. A fountain of blood sprayed onto the man on top of her.

"You bastard!" the man snarled. "You couldn't wait?"

"Finish! Get off! We have to go."

Tentacles of ice spread through Vlad's chest, his whole body.

Goodbye, Papa.

Goodbye, Mama

* * *

Vlad would allow the woman to sleep a few more minutes. Then he would pay her, throw her out.

The dream always made him restless. It was all that was left of his parent's existence.

His father had warned him from the time he was very little—right after they arrived in America—there would be people who would come to kill them. It would happen no matter how hard they tried to hide.

Vlad knew if he was lucky now, he might get away—for a while. But, sooner or later they would find him too.

He had lived with an axe over his head every day since his parents were murdered. He knew the assassins would come. He didn't care anymore.

He dug an elbow into the woman. "Get up! Get out!"

The woman was startled. "Cut it out!" She sprang from the bed, her hair an entangled mess.

In the blink of an eye he was standing up next to her—his fingers raked through her hair and tightened. "What did you say, whore?"

She tried to bow her head. "I'm sorry, Vlad." He released her and she looked at him with pleading eyes, repeated, "I'm sorry."

There was iciness in his chest. It was always there before a kill.

"Please!" She dropped to her knees. "Please, Vlad!"

"Get out of here now before I change my mind."

She grabbed her clothes from a chair, hurried into the bathroom, and was soon dressed and gone.

Vlad thought about the dream again. Thought about his father, who ran from those men in Minsk. It was the same musclemen who forced his father to warehouse drugs. One day, he'd had enough. He refused to live like a criminal. They fled the country and came to live in San Francisco.

There had been no friends, Vlad was homeschooled, and it was a world with only the three of them.

Until the Russians found them.

After that, Vlad lived on the streets, eventually became a hit man for one of the street gangs. When he turned eighteen, he cut himself loose. He didn't like being told what to do. Everyone they sent to teach him a lesson, died a horrible death.

Soon, they stopped trying to kill the Hit Man.

It was also during this time that Vlad found the Pai Gow games in San Francisco's China Town. They were exciting, diverting ... and expensive. Sometimes he had to take on jobs that were not to his liking, but the people who ran the underground Pai Gow games didn't care what he liked or didn't like. Losses were to be paid, or else.

Today, Vlad wondered again why he had that same dream over and over. It was more like a memory file, a visual diary of what happened to his parents—as though it was something he never wanted to forget.

But that would be wrong.

He wanted that memory of being powerless to be erased.

Chapter 8

Gina's classic Fiat Spider was acting up again, sputtering and threatening to die. She tried to give it more gas to keep it alive and moving, but it just ignored her and gave out.

She could feel the heat climbing up her neck. She muttered under her breath, "You nasty little traitor." Harry laughed at her.

"You knew it had to happen sooner or later," Harry said. "It hasn't conked out for months."

She got out of the car, reached into the jump seat for her apron, gloves, and tool box. Armed with her scrubs' protection, she walked to the front and lifted the hood.

"Need a hand, little girl?" Harry said, coming around the car. She knew he was watching her go through her routine—after all, this wasn't the first time she'd been in this situation with her little old lady.

Instead of going through her usual mental check list, she went right to what she thought was causing the problem. And she was right.

She lifted the distributor cap, and said, "Look at that crud." Caked inside was a slew of what looked like hardened green mold. "Why does it keep doing that?"

""Well, if you keep a car outside, it's going to pick up moisture and other junk."

"Harry Lucke, stop talking logic to me at a time like this. Can't you see I'm pissed?"

She looked up at him and when their eyes met they started laughing. "Besides, since when did logic ever have anything to do with my Fiat?"

"You know, doll, we could probably afford a new car, or at least a newer Fiat. I told you about Fiat bringing out a new

124 Spyder after all these years. Maybe we wouldn't have to go through this routine once a week or more."

"She's been behaving for a long time. You said so yourself. Besides, how often do I have to tell you to stop calling me doll." She was almost finished cleaning out the cap. "It sounds sexist and demeaning."

"Right, because you're a woman with dainty little fingers who sits around all day eating chocolates and watching the soaps."

She gave him a bright smile as she closed the hood and restored everything to the back seat. "Just promise you won't do it around anyone else."

"Scout's honor."

She climbed in, hit the ignition, and the car started immediately. She leaned over, wrapped her arms around his neck, and gave him more than a friendly kiss. "I don't know why, but every time you say 'doll,' I want to toss you in the bed and seduce you. So don't do it again."

"Okay, doll."

* * *

The minute Gina stepped into the nurses' station, the team leader said, "Mazzio head on over to the Cath Lab. You're filling in."

"But I've only observed the procedure a couple of times." Her heart was galloping. She didn't like being thrown into new situations, but she wanted to be able to work in any part of Ridgewood's new CCU wing. At least she had *some* training for the Cath Lab.

The team leader was giving her the steely-eyed look.

"Yeah, yeah, I'm on my way."

Gina walked to the far end of the CCU and the minute she walked into the procedure room area, Bob Cantor called to her, "Hi, Gina. Well, well, somebody's watching out for me today. I specifically requested you ... and here you are."

"Thanks, Bob. Hope I can live up to the hype. I've never scrubbed in the Cath Lab before. I've mostly been an observer—so don't expect wonders."

"You'll be fine."

She could see through the glass windows that everything was already set up and the patient was on the table. The circulating nurse looked as though she was talking to the patient and about to give her IV conscious sedation.

Gina let out a huge breath of air to calm herself. The really tricky part—making sure the sterile field had everything that was needed for the procedure—was already done.

Thank God!

Whoever set up had probably already checked to make certain all the equipment was functioning properly, especially the viewing monitors and the floor-to-ceiling image intensifier. Then they would have tested the X-Ray software for recording and playback of the fluoroscopy runs. All of which would have to be ready and available during the procedure.

It was nice to have everything in place, but it still made Gina uneasy. She hoped all the catheters, balloons stents, and everything else were where they were supposed to be under the sheet covering the sterile field. She liked to set up her own sterile fields for any procedure she was scrubbing in for, but the-ready-to-go array really was a gift today.

Gina went into the locker room area and changed into a fresh scrubs, put on her shoe covers and cap, and joined Bob Cantor in the pre-surgical scrub area. Mask on, she also began scrubbing under her nails and skin, brushing methodically and moving slowly up her arms.

"Thanks for sending Lolly Stentz over," he said. "She's not only top notch, she's really nice and easy to work with, even though she has that same funny accent you have."

"You better watch it, Bob. We don't get mad at people who diss us, we just get even."

"Funny, Lolly said the exact same thing. You two must be cloned, even though you have different hair and faces."

"Ha, ha."

"Do you think she likes our office OR and setup? I'd really like to hang onto her if we can," Bob said.

"I don't know." Gina continued to scrub. "I do think she'd rather work only with you."

He blinked and his face flushed under his mask—maybe Bob Cantor also had some concerns of his own about Morton Tallent.

"If my nurse hadn't been with me for the last five years," he said, "I'd say it was a go." His eyes filled with concern. "Is there some kind of problem?"

The circulating nurse stuck her head in. "The patient is juiced and ready."

"Okay, we're there," Bob said, and they were through the door and into the Cath Lab.

Chapter 9

Mort Tallent was jumpy, certain Maria Benke was about to destroy his reputation before she could be silenced. He raced through his hospital rounds, had a hurried lunch, and went to the health club to find Vlad.

Rosia, the large-breasted receptionist, gave him a knowing leer and asked him to have a seat. When she turned around, her shapely ass held his attention until she was out of sight.

She looked familiar—he wondered if she worked for one of the private clubs, like The Madam. He'd only been there once. All of the women there looked alike, with their dark, heavy eye shadow and mascara. But he was always more interested in their bulging breasts and vulva-pinching tights than their faces.

He sat down and in a few moments the woman came back. "He'll be out soon."

Mort ignored her and kept glancing at his watch—if Vlad didn't show up soon he would have to leave for his office appointments without seeing him.

He tried to stay calm, but his stomach was on fire ... bile kept creeping up the back of his throat.

Where the hell is the bastard?

A hand fell on his shoulder, and when he turned his head, Vlad was looking down at him with a pasted-on smile.

"So, Doctor, what can I do for you today? Are you here for one of Vlad's specials?" He curled and straightened his fingers in a way that made Mort cringe.

Mort tried, but he couldn't hide his anger. "You know damn well why I'm here," he said through clenched teeth.

"I make no assumptions."

"You wanted twenty-five grand up front and I gave you what you asked for." Mort had to swallow hard to keep from spitting out the words. "You took the money but you haven't kept your part of our agreement."

Vlad sat down on the bench next to him, placed a hand gently on his thigh, then squeezed the muscles so hard Mort's leg went numb.

Fear replaced anger.

"You remember when I handled that problem you had with your wife?" Vlad's hand never let up. Mort wanted to cry out, couldn't dare. "I took care of it in my own way, in my own time, Doctor. Remember?"

Vlad finally let go of Mort's leg. He could breathe again.

"I don't want the woman to open her mouth and talk to the others," Mort said softly. "If that happens, I'm finished."

Vlad ignored him. "It looks like our little receptionist has eyes for you, Doc. Maybe I could arrange a little session, strictly professional, you know. She has a way of satisfying and easing those unnecessary fears."

Mort looked at the woman. She was smiling and running her tongue lightly over her lips. His buttocks clenched. He felt himself getting hard.

"I have to get back to the office." He stood and turned away. "We need to take care of this business now or there could be problems for *both* of us."

He could feel Vlad's eyes burning a hole in his back as he hurried away.

* * *

Gina lifted her iPhone from her pocket, hoped it was Harry calling from ICU. It was Lolly. She exhaled a deep breath.

She didn't want to talk to her friend right now. Things had gone really well in the Cath Lab. She'd needed more prompting than she would have preferred, but Bob Cantor was great. He explained each step in the procedure. Right off he'd shown Gina how to a set a sheath so a hollow catheter could enter the artery. It was fascinating, and she hadn't screwed up once.

"Hi, Lolly."

"Got a minute?"

"Um, yeah, but only a minute."

"Listen, this is the second day Maria hasn't come to work. I'm really worried about her."

"Maybe she has the flu," Gina said. "Cases are starting to pop up. I mean she could be sick."

"I have a bad feeling about this, Gina. It's been that way right from the moment she told me about Mort Tallent's scamming. He seems like such an unsavory kind of guy. He gives me the creeps the way he looks at me."

"Have you tried calling Maria?"

"I don't want to scare her more than she probably is already," Lolly said. "It's a shame that Tallent's working with two great partners. It's not fair to them. You know as well as I do that if Tallent goes down it's going to really ruin the whole practice."

"Yeah. Guilty by association. That would be horrible." Gina paused for a moment, then said, "Try to call her. See what she says. Then we'll talk. Okay?"

* * *

Throughout the day, Maria's mother kept saying, "Why no work?"

"I'm not feeling well, Ma."

Her mother didn't believe her, kept shaking her head.

Maria really wasn't a good liar, and she'd be the first to admit it. She had tons of sick time accumulated because she couldn't lie. Pretending to be ill wasn't an option. Not for her— no one would believe her.

The phone rang.

She checked the window on the telephone. It was Lolly Stentz.

Oh, damn!

Her mother called out, "Get the phone, Maria!"

"Okay, okay, I'm getting it."

She snatched up the phone. "Hello?"

"Hi, Maria. It's me, Lolly, from work."

"Oh, hi, Lolly."

There was long pause before the nurse spoke. "Are you all right?"

"Just not feeling well." Maria could hear her voice and was certain that anybody who knew her would be aware she was lying. But she'd been around Lolly for only a short time. Maybe she would believe her.

"After what we discussed, I was worried."

She knew Lolly was still at work, not only because of the hour, but because the nurse had lowered her voice until it was almost a whisper.

"Maybe I was overreacting. I shouldn't have brought you into it. We can talk about it when I come back to work. Just as soon as I feel better."

There was no response.

"Lolly?"

"I'm here."

Maria swallowed hard. "I'll see you soon. Okay?"

"Okay."

Chapter 10

Maria Benke dropped a half-dozen large, homemade dumplings into the chicken stew simmering on the kitchen stove. The stew was a variation on a German recipe that had been in the family for generations, and one of her mother's favorites. When she was sure the dumplings were thoroughly cooked, she set up two small folding tables in the living room so she and her mother could eat and watch the Bill Maher television show.

They watched and laughed while they ate, taking two helpings each. It was a Friday night routine.

Mrs. Benke still had to use a walker to get around the house, but in the past couple of months, she'd more and more refused any offers of help. She was even pushing herself out of bed and getting dressed on her own.

Now that her mother was getting around the apartment fairly well on her own, they no longer needed caretakers for daytime assistance. Maria was pleased to see her mother regaining her strength and confidence.

It had been a long haul and Maria was starting to relax a little. She realized that perhaps she'd overreacted to Dr. Tallent's nasty response when she'd asked him about his bookkeeping accounts. The man had always been difficult to work within the best of times. She decided she would return to work tomorrow and scope out the situation. If things looked like they weren't going to work out for her, she would start looking for a new job.

Can't hide out here at home forever.

When the TV show was over, she helped her mother with a bath and getting back into bed. She cleaned up in the living room, put the trays away, and stashed their plates and silverware in the dishwasher.

She did a few reach-for-the-ceiling stretches to ease her back, then turned to leave the kitchen.

A man she'd never seen before was standing next to the refrigerator, smiling.

She jumped back, her hand flew to her mouth, and she let out an ear-piercing scream. Her legs wouldn't hold her and she stumbled back to crash against the edge of the counter.

"Maria!" her mother called out. "Are you awright?"

"Who are you?" Maria said, grasping the counter to keep from collapsing on the floor. "How did you get in here?"

He scrutinized her like someone standing over a package of meat in the supermarket. He tilted his head to the side, continued to focus on her with eyes that did not reflect his smile.

"What do you want?" She tried to regain strength in her legs. "Get out of here!" She reached for the wood knife block on the center counter and pulled out a long carving knife.

The man, dressed in chino pants, plaid shirt, gimme hat, and sneakers, looked her up and down, then leaned against the refrigerator and laughed mirthlessly.

"What do you want?" she repeated, her voice trembling.

"I want you to die."

She gasped, her chest constricted, and she began to shake.

"Maria!" Her mother again.

He took a step toward her. She wanted to run, but her legs still wouldn't move. He kept coming and didn't stop until he was smack up against her. One arm curled around her waist, held her in a vice-like grip while he used his other hand to grasp the top of her head. He squeezed and forced her face against his chest.

She dropped the knife, flailed at him with both fists.

"Now, now, Maria! You can't fight me with those puny muscles of yours." He bent her back over the counter, down hard on her neck. She screamed again.

"Maria?" Louder this time.

He covered her mouth, thrust a hand up between her legs, lifted her off her feet, and carried her into the living room. When he tossed her onto the floor, it felt like her back had shattered. She couldn't move.

"Maria! Whas a madder?" her mother called out from the bedroom.

Maria looked up at him. He never said a word. He just stared at her with eyes that were like wet stone.

She croaked out, "Nothing, mom. Everything's okay."

Her cell rang. He took it from the coffee table and handed it to her. The window said it was Lolly Stentz. Maria looked at the man. He nodded and she pressed the speaker button.

"Hello?"

"Hi, Maria. Hope I'm not bothering you. Don't know why, but I felt a need to call you again ... see how you are."

"I'm ... I'm better."

"Do you need anything? I'd be happy to come over and keep you company for awhile. I'm worried about you."

"No, I'm all right. I'm coming in to work tomorrow. I'll see you then."

"Really? I don't know. You don't sound like yourself."

"It's ... it's just getting late and I'm tired. That's all."

"Well, okay. Call me if you need anything."

Maria clicked off and started crying.

* * *

Vlad Folo looked down at the helpless woman. He knew she was terrified, out of her mind with fear.

He felt nothing. There was only that iciness sitting in the middle of his chest, freezing his insides, like always.

This was a job and he would do what he had to do. Actions born of the same necessity that had turned him into a surviving orphan.

When those men killed his family and left the apartment, he'd crept out of the closet, looked down at the bodies. His father's face was contorted, eyes staring at nothingness; his mother's body slack and battered.

Both were bathed in blood.

Something told him he should cry. But his insides were cold, numb, and dead ... as they were now.

He picked the woman up from the floor—she was very, very light, as if she didn't really exist. She must have been in pain because she had bitten her lip so hard that blood had welled up between her teeth..

He carried her into what he assumed was her room, laid her on the bed. Her eyes never left his face. She watched his every move, watched him as he took a knife from his pocket and sliced off her clothes, watched while he took off his own clothes and stuffed his underwear into her mouth. He stood over her, stared at her tiny breasts and small, round belly. She tried to move, her face creased with agony, but she was helpless.

He wanted to imagine the pain she was feeling, understand the pain his parents must have felt. How would it feel to have this kind of fear crashing everywhere inside your trapped body?

But he felt nothing.

He crouched down, spread and lifted her legs, listened as she grunted in pain. Only her cloth-stuffed mouth held back her screams. When he entered her, he felt the rush of heat inside her body.

But the rest of him felt nothing, not even when he slashed her throat.

Chapter 11

"So, guys, you think April would be a good time of our wonderful double wedding?" Helen said. "Or is that too soon?"

"Gives us six months to work out all the details," Gina said. Dinner was over and they were sitting in the living room. Harry and Vinnie nodded their agreement.

"It's not a whole lot of time, but then we're not planning a big bash," Harry said. "Just a few friends, right?"

Vinnie, sitting next to Helen, scowled, looked over at his sister. "We're gonna have to invite Mom and Dad, Gina. You know that."

Gina knew he was right ... and hated him for it. She was beginning to regret that she and

Harry agreed to a double wedding with Vinnie and Helen.

"I don't care what's right," she said. "They never supported my leaving Dominick—they wanted me to stay in that horrible marriage because they were friends with his parents." She jumped up and paced around the living room. Helen, sitting next to Vinnie, looked perplexed.

"Come back and sit next to me," Harry said. "Come on, doll. It's okay."

Gina slid back onto the love seat; Harry took her hand. "You're first generation American, your parents came here looking for a new life, and they—"

"—I know all that stuff, Harry. I'm tired of hearing it. It all sounds so logical and understandable while we're comfortably sitting here talking in our living room. But the reality? My parents were awful to me. Even after all this time, I can't forgive them."

"Maybe this is what we need to mend those fences," Vinnie said. "For four years Mom and Dad kept asking about you. Mom, in particular, is really depressed about your being gone."

"Yeah, but is she sad enough to apologize?" Gina stared hard at Vinnie. "I doubt it."

Helen, always the mediator, said, "I never thought I would ever say this, but I'm lucky not to have this kind of problem—sometimes being an orphan is a blessing."

"It's not going to be a picnic with *my* family, either." Harry said. "They still call you 'The little Catholic girl.' Not Gina. No, *the little Catholic girl*. It makes me furious. Do you think I want them at our wedding with that attitude?"

"Face it, big sister," Vinnie said softly, "you're going to have to forgive them sooner or later. And what better opportunity than this?"

Gina leaned back into Harry. "Let's elope."

"I'd love to. But that won't make the problem go away. You know Vinnie's right. It's time to forgive them."

Gina's phone buzzed. She looked at it and said, "It's Lolly. I'd better take it." She stepped out of the living room and caught the call on the fourth ring.

"Hi, Lolly, what's up?"

"It's me, the pest." There was a long pause. "I know you think I'm crazy, but I can't help it. I'm worried about Mort Tallent's bookkeeper."

"Silly, I don't think you're crazy ... you have a big heart, Lolly. That's what I love about you. Have you tried calling her?"

"That's it. I have. I tried yesterday and it went to messages. Spoke to her earlier and decided to call again. Tonight, when she picked up, she sounded really weird."

"Weird? In what way?" Gina asked.

"Scared—I know scared when I hear it—she was definitely scared."

"What do you want to do?"

There was a long moment before Lolly said, "Would you and Harry mind going over to her apartment with me ... just to see how she's doing? We'd only have to say hi, then go. Maybe I'll sleep better tonight."

It was definitely bad timing. One way or another Gina knew she would have to settle this business about her mother and father with Vinnie. Well, it was going to be later than sooner. "You'll have to pick us up. We only have a two-seater. Harry's car is stowed away in the garage."

* * *

"Harry and I have to go with Lolly to check up on a friend," Gina said, putting on her jacket.

"You just want to get out of this whole business with Mom and Dad." She could see Vinnie was totally frustrated with her attitude. "You know we need to iron this out."

"We'll talk about it another time," Harry said.

Helen turned to Vinnie. "We'll get to it. Just not tonight."

"That was the point. Tonight was supposed to be the night to settle it once and for all."

"We're not going to let a friend down now because we're busy planning our future," Harry said. "It sounds like Lolly needs us now."

"In case you didn't know it, that's what friends do for each other," Gina said.

Vinnie was up and in her face. "Yeah, and what do people do for their families?"

Gina turned her back on him.

"Let's wait outside," she said to Harry.

* * *

The three of them sat in Lolly's Honda Civic, parked outside Maria Benke's apartment house. They sat in silence, staring at the smoked-glass façade. Gina could see a doorman in the lobby, sitting behind a small desk.

"This is a pretty posh place," Lolly said. "I knew I should have gone into something other than nursing."

Harry laughed. "If you'd become a bookkeeper like Maria, you'd be staring at numbers all day long. I know I wouldn't like it; I'd go crazy in less than a week."

"I don't know if that's true for me," Gina said. She rolled up her window "Numbers are a helluva lot less complicated than people."

"Unless you can't do arithmetic." Harry bent over and kissed her. "And you can't."

"Very funny. I could still cancel the wedding, you know?"

"Okay, I take it back."

"Now that we're actually here, I feel kind of silly," Lolly said. "Do you think I'm just being a busybody interfering in her life?"

"Lolly, I trust your intuition, and you should, too. You've always been as nutty as I am." Gina pressed down on the door handle. "If you think there's something wrong, we ought to look into it."

* * *

When they came through the door and headed for the first floor apartment, the doorman hardly looked up from a book he'd half hidden under papers at the edge of the desk.

"Not much challenge there. We could have been thieves in the night. As long as we were dressed decently we would have made it in," Gina said, looking at the top of the doorman's head.

"The guy's just putting in his hours and collecting a check." Harry started walking to the elevator. "To his credit, he *is* reading a book."

Outside of Maria's apartment, they hesitated.

Gina's scalp was tingling. She knew something was wrong when she reached out and rang the bell. After several seconds, she rang it again.

Harry tried the door handle. "It's not locked." They looked at each other in surprise, then stepped inside.

Every light in the apartment appeared to be on. "Hello," Gina said. She walked through the small foyer; the others were right behind her.

The living room was a mess—things scattered everywhere.

"Maria!" Lolly called out.

Gina sniffed at the air. That rank combination of sweat, fear, and blood surrounded them. "We need to check the rooms."

They moved down the hall and crowded into the first bedroom.

"Oh, my God!" Lolly cried out. "It's Maria."

Blood was spattered everywhere. Maria was tied down to the bed and her mouth was stuffed with a rag. But that wasn't the worst of it—or was it her helplessness, lying in puddles of body fluids that were congealing all around her.

No, it wasn't that.

It was her eyes. They were open and vacant. They seemed to be saying:

Look at me. Look what they've done to me.

Bette Golden Lamb & J. J. Lamb

Chapter 12

When the police arrived at Maria's apartment, they asked Lolly, Gina, and Harry a few preliminary questions, then told them to wait in the living room.

It was more than thirty minutes before an Inspector Trowbred finally came out and started questioning them more seriously.

"So, Ms. Stentz, I know you said you worked with Ms. Benke. Did you know both victims?"

"Both victims?" Gina said.

"Well, there's an older women in the back bedroom. You didn't know that?"

"Inspector, we didn't think about there being other victims," Harry said. "We saw Maria, immediately dialed 911, and waited. That was it."

"Gina and Harry came with me," Lolly said, "because I asked them to. But I wasn't aware there was anyone else was living with Maria. I knew her mother had suffered a stroke. I assumed she was living in a rehab facility."

"But you did work with her?"

"I've only been at the job for two months. I haven't had a chance to get to know *anyone* really well."

"From identification in the second victim's wallet, it was probably Ms. Benke's mother." The inspector seemed really annoyed with them. "There's a walker in there and a lot of other medical paraphernalia."

"Do you mind if we take a look?" Harry said. "We might be able to help. The three of us are nurses; we probably could help identify any medical problems she had."

"I was hoping Mulzini might be on call." Gina forced a smile. "He's a friend of ours."

The inspector chuckled. "You know that pain in the ass Mulzini?"

"Yes."

The inspector lost his smile. "He's been out on sick leave for the last couple of weeks."

"What's wrong?" Harry said.

The inspector became jittery. "I don't know. They don't tell us anything. I called the schlub, but he was tight-lipped about the whole business." The inspector looked at the three of them. "All right, come on back. Let me know what you think of her medical status. Otherwise, by the time the MEs finish, the killer could be half way around the world."

They walked past the bedroom where Maria was, continued on around a corner and into the other bedroom.

Gina whispered in Harry's ear, "I can see why we missed it with that turn in the hall."

Harry nodded. "I don't think any of us wanted to do any more looking around after we found Maria's body." He gave Gina a don't-say-a-word look.

Outside the bedroom door, the inspector said, "Now don't freak out on me. It's really bad in there."

When they walked inside, Gina's throat closed. That was a good thing because the scene was a nightmare, enough to make anyone barf. Both Gina and Lolly grabbed Harry and held on for dear life.

Like Maria, the woman had something stuffed into her mouth. Also, her hands and feet were bound. There was blood everywhere and the metallic smell permeated the room, but unlike Maria, this woman's trail of blood started at a vertical slice through her lips that continued down her whole torso.

Her neck had been slashed too, but instead of a smooth slice like Maria's, this cut had been slow and jagged.

"It looks like she was alive up until her carotid was severed," Harry said to the inspector.

"Yeah, I think the bastard raped and tortured her before he finished her off."

Gina edged to the bed stand and looked at the bottles of medications. She lifted each one and read the label. "Considering her age and her medications, plus the equipment and the kind of books she was reading, I think she was most likely recovering from a stroke."

Harry and Lolly agreed.

Gina was compelled to look into the woman's eyes, just as she had with Maria, whose eyes had reflected horror.

Her mother's eyes told a different story.

Gina saw only resignation.

Chapter 13

Vlad looked intently at the filet mignon the waiter placed in front of him. He cut into the center with surgical precision. It was rare, just the way he liked it, and he nodded at the waiting server. He sliced off a large piece for his first bite, chewed slowly, and savored it.

Perfection.

He always ate at Rizzo's after a kill. Here, everything would be as exceptional as he was. After all, he did his job well—he expected the same from others.

He'd come here right after the hit—after killing Tallent's target, Maria Benke. Her mother was only collateral damage control—a loose string he'd had to cut away.

Chewing the steak, he visualized how he'd finished the hit with a final slash across Maria's neck.

Bloody and naked, he'd gone down the hall, knife in hand, the same one he'd used on Maria. He walked into the mother's room which was heavy with the odors and messiness of some kind of sickness—the stink of decay.

The first thing he did was check the woman's closet, the way he had her daughter's. There would be no witnesses when he was finished.

His parents' murderers had been sloppy. They'd left Vlad behind to remember, cling to every single detail of the crime—the death scene was seared in his brain forever.

Maria's mother had looked at his naked body. He watched the fight go out of her when he placed the knife on the bedside table. Her gaze followed his every move as he advanced from closet to dresser, where he rummaged through all the drawers before pulling out one of her nightgowns. He carefully cut it into strips with his bloody knife to tie her hands and ankles.

She'd offered no resistance when his hands moved up and down her old and wrinkled body, or when he lashed her to the bed. He wanted to toy with her, the way he had with Maria, but her lack of movement, her complete surrender didn't inspire his sense of perfection.

Vlad pictured his mother trying to move her hips away, fight the thrust of her attacker. But when Vlad pushed himself inside Maria's mother, she remained so limp she might as well have been a corpse already.

Tears gushed down her cheeks when he grabbed the knife from the table and started slicing from her mouth on down.

She didn't scream; she didn't even whimper.

Annoyed, he'd slowly cut across her neck to make her suffer. But when her blood flew up like a geyser spraying the air, her eyes remained steady and fearless.

Vlad didn't like that memory. He pushed his plate away, with its half-eaten steak.

"Is there something wrong, sir?" the waiter said, hurrying to the table.

"No! Just take it away and bring me a double Stolie. Make sure it's ice-cold."

"Yes, sir."

He caught a cab to Chinatown and went directly to his favorite Pai Gow game. It was not a good decision. When he finally came back out to Grant Avenue. The owners of the game were holding his chit for $10,000.

Not a good decision at all.

* * *

None of them had spoken during the cross-town drive. Now, the three of them still sat silently in Lolly's Honda outside Gina and Harry's apartment building. All the happiness and optimism Gina had felt earlier was stripped away—she felt wasted and empty

"Come inside, Lolly," Gina finally said. She could barely feel her lips move. "Let's have some coffee and talk for a while."

Lolly started crying; she covered her face with her hands. "I don't want to talk about it right now. I keep thinking that if we'd gone to see her sooner, we might have saved her."

"Come on, Lolly, it's not your fault," Harry said. "It is what it is."

"Please don't say that, Harry," Gina said. "You know how much I hate that meaningless expression."

"Don't like it much myself, doll. But it fits the situation." He reached between the front seats and squeezed her arm. "There was nothing we could have done to save her."

"It was all so strange. I knew she was afraid of Tallent," Lolly said. "She was frantic and convinced she might be murdered. She made me uneasy and I was scared when I came to you. But deep down, I never really dreamed someone would actually kill her." Lolly wiped away tears and blew her nose. "I tried to tell myself that what she was really afraid of, was being fired."

"Mort Tallent has a reputation for being a badass," Gina said. "But in the short time I've been in CCU, he's been one of the calmest people I've ever worked with. Even when I screwed up one of his NPO orders."

"You didn't?" Lolly said.

"The time you fed a patient before a procedure, right?" Harry said.

"That's the one. They had to put off a trip to the Cath Lab that day because of me," Gina said. "In my defense, the bed chart had nothing on it about NPO and I missed it in the nurses' notes. So I gave her breakfast."

"What did Tallent do?" Lolly asked.

"Well, I expected him to rant and rave. I mean, I had it coming, and he's not known to be understanding with the nursing staff. But he was truly nice about it." Gina said. "I was shocked, but, you know, why look a gift horse in the mouth?"

"Me, I dread going to work tomorrow," Lolly said. "Now I have to find an opportunity to take a look at the office files."

"You can't do that, Lolly," Gina said. "You could end up dead, too."

"How else are we going to find out what it was Maria saw, what she was so afraid of?"

"There has to be a way to get to the truth," Gina said.

"Just a minute!" Harry barked. "You're not getting involved in this, Gina Mazzio. Have you forgotten how you almost got killed a year ago sticking your nose into other people's business?"

"Stop it! You make me sound like some old busybody. I only got into trouble because people needed help."

"But why do you always have to be the one to go looking for the answers?" Harry's hair was flying every which way, his voice was rising, and he was half out of his seat.

"I'm sorry I got you two into this mess," Lolly said. "I didn't know who to turn to."

"Don't worry about it," Gina said. She took a long moment to think. "Do you really think you can get into the office's bookkeeping files without getting caught? Or Tallent's private files?"

"Very risky."

"Gina, you're doing it again," Harry said. "Back off! This isn't your fight."

Lolly looked at Harry, then back at Gina. "I'll let you know what I find out."

Chapter 14

Mort Tallent showed his "Do it" chip to the man dressed in a tux at the doorway. The name of the club had intrigued him ever since Vlad told him about it a couple of months ago. What Vlad didn't tell him about was the hefty fee Tallent would have to pay up front if he wanted to join.

"Anything worth doing comes at a price," his dad would have said.

He stepped through the doorway onto plush burgundy carpeting. A tall, gorgeous brunette immediately laced her arm through his.

"Good evening, sir," she said in an almost-but-not-quite sultry voice.

"Hello."

He didn't really know what to do next. He'd never been to an S&M club—didn't even know if it was something he wanted to do. But after Vlad called and said that Maria would no longer be a problem, he was determined to celebrate his freedom with something new and different.

The woman led him into a dimly lighted dressing room; the walls and the ceiling were covered with mirrors. There was no one else in the room.

"Please remove all of your clothing and slip into this," his escort said, offering him a black suede loincloth. "Someone will come for you in a few minutes." She smiled and walked out.

He was beginning to think this was a dumb idea, but everything he'd done this night had been to keep Maria's face from flashing in his head. He'd already downed an entire bottle of Merlot without feeling even the slightest buzz.

He couldn't stop thinking about Maria, wondering if she had suffered. He hadn't wanted her to feel pain.

I liked her. She should have kept her nose out of my affairs. It was all her own fault.

He stripped. Since there was no place for him to put his clothes, he laid them neatly on the floor and put on the soft loincloth.

He looked at himself in the mirrors. For the first time, he admitted to himself that he looked every single day of his fifty-five years. Maybe older. When did his paunch get so big and the muscles in his arms so small? And what happened to his chest? His *pecs*?

Pectoralis major. In my case, minor, very minor. God, how I've let myself go to seed.

Well, at least he still had that bushy crop of hair on the top of his head even though the streaks of gray were turning into wide roadways.

What the hell am I doing here anyway?

He was about to shed the loincloth, get dressed again, and walk out of the club when another voluptuous female, this one a redhead, came into the room through one of the mirrored doorways. She was totally naked, except for five-inch heels. No question, she was a natural redhead. He gulped several times and wanted to cross his hands across the front of the loincloth, which was starting to push out.

"Madame Catcora is waiting for you." She placed a hand gently on his forearm and led him back through the doorway. He walked obediently along side of her despite a strong desire to cut and run.

"Where are we going?"

"As I said—to Madame Catcora." Her voice was very soft.

Tallent was now in a torch-lit hallway that ramped sharply downward. They walked for what seemed like forever before entering a small room that was even dimmer than the hallway and glass-paneled dressing room.

Standing in front of him on a raised platform was a woman in a black bodice corset that extended from her breasts to her hips. Her legs were very long and seemed to go on forever before ending with narrow feet inside a pair of glittering silver shoes with spiked heels. He couldn't see her face. Once again he wanted to turn away, run, but he couldn't do anything other than stare at the hairless vulva that was right in front of his eyes.

"Come over here!" She pointed to a specific spot with the end of a whip that was silver, like her shoes.

Again, all he wanted to do was run, but his legs betrayed him and carried him to the designated spot.

As he moved forward, he noticed another man in the room, dressed the same as Tallent. The man's eyes were wide open and his expression said that he, too, wanted to escape.

Madame Catcora seemed to float down from the platform; her black mascara-coated eyes made her look like a demon. With the heels, she must have been six-five or so. She walked up to the other man, bent slightly at the waist, licked his face, and moved down to suck his nipples.

"Tie him up!" she ordered.

A huge, buff man, also dressed in a loincloth, stepped out of the darkness. An overhead soft spotlight followed him as he tugged the man to a scaffold and slipped his wrists into cuffs that were chained to the framework. A swift yank also pulled away the loin cloth.

Without a word, Madame Catcora began to lash him with her short whip, gently at first, then with more and more force until he cried out for her to stop.

She moved closer, licked his face again. "What's the matter, little man?"

Madame Catcora waited for an answer that never came.

It was only then that Tallent noticed the man had an enormous erection. He couldn't take his eyes off of it, watched intently as the woman ran one hand up the man's thigh and let it come to rest on his buttock.

With her other hand, she reached out and removed a huge dildo from the drawer of a stand next to the scaffold. She held it in front of his face, wiggled it a couple of times, and squeezed his buttock. "Isn't this what you've been waiting for?"

Mort Tallent turned around, ran from the room, up the ramp, and into the mirrored dressing room. Half-dressed, he raced out of the club as though demons were chasing him.

Chapter 15

The next day, during her lunch break, Gina found a quiet corner in the nurses' lounge and sipped at a cup of coffee. She'd added more half-and-half than she should have, along with two teaspoons of sugar. It was like having a low-calorie desert.

It was one of those days.

The chair she'd snagged was almost too comfortable, like almost everything in the new CCU wing. She pulled out her cell and hit the button for Inspector Mulzini. After the fourth ring, he picked up.

"Yeah?"

"Hi, Mulzini. Um, you sound like you're ripping mad. If this is a bad time, I'll call back later."

"If I hadn't seen your goofy name, Mazzio, I wouldn't have picked up. I'm not in the mood to talk too much of anybody lately. What's it been, a year since I last saw you?"

"Yep. Been no hot water for you to pull me out of lately."

"A whole year, huh?"

"Something like that." She paused for a moment before adding, "Rumor has it that you've been out sick for a couple of weeks."

"Yeah, so what? I've got months of sick leave coming. And that's exactly what I told Harry when he called."

"Well, you don't have to chew my head off. We're concerned about you."

The phone went quiet for a long time. Gina began to think he'd hung up on her.

"Sorry, Mazzio, guess I sound like a nut, but just between you and me, I've got an appointment with a doc tomorrow and I'm ... I'm kinda scared."

"Oh, Mulzini! I'm so sorry." She held her breath for a moment, trying to squash her own fears for her friend. "If you don't mind my asking, what's going on?"

Another long silence.

Mulzini had always been pretty much up front with her from the first day they'd met four years ago, but now he was holding back. If the inspector in charge of Maria Benke and her mother's murders hadn't said something at the crime scene about Mulzini, she'd have been in the dark altogether. It had to be something big to keep that workaholic away from the job.

"Listen, you and I have been friends since I came to California," Gina said. "You're my go-to guy in law enforcement. When I heard you'd been out sick for two weeks, I was ... was worried. You can't blame me for that, can you?"

"It's my ticker."

"Your heart? What about it?" She was fighting hard to remain calm, but she couldn't help it—she was scared.

"Well, my doc had me on meds for atrial fibrillation— man, that's some mouth full, isn't it? Anyway, the meds aren't working, in fact, it's been getting worse. So I'm going to see a cardiologist tomorrow. See what he thinks."

"How long has this been going on?" Gina's hands were shaking when she took a sip of her coffee. "You never said a word about it the last time I saw you."

"Yeah, well, it's been about a year. Give or take. It wasn't long after I last saw you."

"Will you do me a favor, please? Keep me in the loop. I know we don't see each other often, but next to Harry, you're my favorite guy."

"I know you—that's just talk. There is no next to Harry. Lucky dog!"

"Who are you going to see tomorrow?"

"I've got the guy's name on the appointment card in my jacket pocket. The doc I was recommended to didn't have any openings. I would have had to wait two more weeks to get in.

They're all alike to me. I got in almost right away with his partner."

Gina's eye started twitching and she was getting a weird feeling in the bottom of her stomach.

"Hey, Mulzini. I hate turning nurse on you, but would you mind getting that appointment card? I'd like to know who you're going to see."

"I swear you're a bad as my wife. Marcia also has to know every single damn detail. Hang on a minute." She could tell he was breathing heavily when he returned to the phone.

"Work a man to death. It's a guy named Morton Tallent.

* * *

Gina hit Harry's cell phone number and waited impatiently while it rang. She knew it was about to go to message mode when he finally picked up.

"Hey, doll, what's going on? I'm kind of in the middle of something, got only a minute or two to talk."

"I spoke to Mulzini."

"Yeah, I called him, too," Harry said. "What a bear. He practically tore my head off."

"He wasn't too pleasant to me, either. The poor guy is scared."

"He told me about his atrial fib," Harry said. "My bet is that they'll do an ablation."

"I'm really worried about him. You'll never guess who he has an appointment with tomorrow."

"I didn't get that far with him," Harry said. "Probably a cardiologist."

"Yeah, but it's with Mort Tallent."

"Oh, shit!"

Bette Golden Lamb & J. J. Lamb

Chapter 16

Lolly had gone to work that day prepared to remain silent, not say a word about the deaths of Maria and her mother. But everyone at the offices of Tallent, Brichett, and Cantor already knew about it and were in a state of shock. Word had spread like wildfire after a couple of the staff members saw it online.

Lolly kept her thoughts to herself but when the doctors held a meeting with the staff to talk about it, she studied Mort Tallent's face very closely. He seemed as pale and as shaken as every other person in the room.

Robert Cantor did most of the talking.

"This has been an awful shock for all of us," Cantor said in a somber voice to those gathered in the reception area. "We can't imagine why anyone would do something so awful to one of the nicest people I've ever known."

"And her mother, too," Jon Brichett said. "It's beyond belief."

"I wish we could close the offices today," Cantor said. "And perhaps you may think this sounds insensitive, but most of the patients scheduled for procedures are already prepped and medicated. As you all know, this not a segment of the population that does particularly well with stress. Delaying their procedures would only make things worse. We simply can't do that."

Lolly kept watching Mort Tallent. He remained silent and constantly dabbed at his forehead with a handkerchief. But his face never lost its sheen of sweat.

"However, if anyone wants to take the day off, we'll respect that request," Brichett said. "If so, please raise your hand now."

The room was deadly silent. Lolly could hear her own heart thrumming in her ears. Throughout the night, images of

Maria and her mother's naked, cut-up bodies kept flashing in her brain. Maria had been right to be frightened.

My, God! Tallent's books must be horribly damaging.

And although there was nothing to pin him to the two women's deaths, Lolly had no doubt that in some way Mort Tallent was behind the slaughter of Maria and her mother.

* * *

"You have to go with me," Lolly said to Gina. "I can't do this myself."

"You want to break into the offices?" Gina squeezed the phone tighter, knew right then and there that she should hang up on her friend. "Lolly, we can't do that."

"I spent the whole day, like said I would, trying to get into the bookkeeping files without being seen. No deal. There was somebody around every minute. Besides, it won't be a true break-in—I have keys that unlock everything. We just walk in, take a look around, and leave. Who's to know?"

Gina took a long time to consider what her friend was asking.

"Are you still there, Gina?"

"Listen, Lolly, I've been in way too much trouble in the past. It's really been nice spending this last year minding my own business, staying out of trouble, and having more time with Harry. Now you come along and start talking about breaking into offices in the middle of the night."

"I guess that's it in a nutshell."

"Why? Just on the off chance we might find whatever it was that Maria found?" But the wheels started turning and her curiosity was kicking in. She could feel herself tapping one toe on a very slippery slope.

"The idea of that miserable man killing Maria, really gets my Bronx up, ya know?" Lolly said.

"Well, we're not in the Bronx," Gina snapped back. "Besides, I can't buy Mort Tallent killing any one, much less two people."

"I don't really think Tallent did it. I think he probably hired someone to do it."

Gina glanced toward the bathroom. Harry had been in the shower when Lolly's call came in. She could still hear the water running as she sat on the edge of their bed and thought long and hard about Tallent and Lolly's request.

She knew she should step back. This was definitely not the kind of thing she should stick her nose into. Instead, she said, "Okay, Lolly, I'll go with you, more to keep you out of trouble than anything else."

"Thanks, Gina. I owe you one. A big one."

"Man, if Harry finds out about this, he's going to kill me."

* * *

Gina and Lolly decided to wear scrubs in case something went wrong—they could at least try to make it look like they belonged in the place.

Although Lolly had been a springboard for the whole thing, she admitted to Gina that she was terrified just by the thought that they were going to Tallent, Cantor, & Brichett at two in the morning. True to her word, though, she had the key.

"They gave it to me so I could get in and get things ready when one of them had an early case."

While hospitals rigidly stuck to schedules, except for emergencies, private offices had to be more flexible for their patients' convenience. Sometimes procedures started much earlier or later than they did in hospitals.

Gina had to force herself to climb into Lolly's Honda Civic. "It's a good thing Harry sleeps like there's no tomorrow, or sneaking out would have been impossible."

After that they were silent as they rode through the deserted streets. At this hour, San Francisco had a beauty that was difficult to resist. As she had done so many times, Gina recognized that she no longer had any regrets about leaving the Bronx. That chapter of her life was over and done with.

She'd enjoyed working for Jacoby Hospital all those years, but knew Lolly was here only to get away from all of the friends who were constantly chiding her about finding a guy and settling down. She obviously liked being independent and living on her own.

Lolly parked the car and used her key-card to enter the building. She had to use it again to activate the elevator to reach the offices, in-house procedure rooms, and the care unit in the penthouse.

"Everyone was a come-and-go case today, so the floor should be deserted," she whispered to Gina.

They tiptoed through the silent reception area, with its scattered night lights, and went directly to Mort Tallent's office. The door was open. They went inside and straight to his desk where a dim overhead spotlight illuminated the area.

His computer screen had a green caduceus icon dead center as wallpaper. "No doubt password protected" Gina said. "Know what it is?"

"Damn! I didn't think about that."

Before they could touch anything, Gina saw a back-and-forth moving light bouncing off the hallway rug. They both dropped to their knees behind the desk. Gina was hyperventilating; she concentrated hard on slowing down her breathing.

Whoever it was out there was whistling.

Security?

"Must be the building's night watchman," Lolly whispered.

"Oh, my God! Does he know you?"

"No." Lolly could barely get the words out. "Don't think we've ever run into each other."

Gina shook her head and glared at her friend.

How could I be so stupid? Should have known someone would be checking the building at night. This is the dumbest thing I've ever done.

Chapter 17

The night light in the office was dim, but it felt like the brightest spotlight Gina had ever been under. They were both huddled together and Gina could feel her friend trembling when the whistling watchman's light flashed briefly into Mort Tallent's office before moving on.

The Beatle's *We All Live In A Yellow Submarine* bounced off the walls of the hallway for another few minutes before everything was silent again. The two of them collapsed into each other's arms before they stood.

"Okay," Gina whispered. "Do you have any idea what his password might be?"

"Not a clue."

"Let's take a look in his desk drawer. Sometimes people will write it down on something in case they forget." Gina pulled open the middle drawer while Lolly opened one on the left-hand side. "Look for accounting books, too."

Gina picked up a red chip. Etched boldly in the middle were the words, *Do it!*

"I wonder what this is from." She showed to Lolly, who only shrugged.

In the back of the drawer was a gold membership card to *Time Out,* a posh health club Gina vaguely remembered hearing about. Otherwise, the drawer was filled with an assortment of paper clips and Post-its. Tallent seem to be compulsive from the looks of this drawer and the top of the desk, where everything was stacked in several neat piles.

Lolly found a pad with columns of hand written numbers, but they looked like private accounting numbers—the long list didn't look right for a pass word.

The rest of the drawers had neither accounting books nor much of anything else.

Gina tossed the health club membership card back into the drawer; it flipped over to reveal a small, pencil-written notation. She found a magnifying glass, with Zelint's Pharmaceuticals molded into the plastic handle, and read:

ANNIE'S DOWN

"I wonder who Annie is." Gina said. "Do you know?"

Lolly shrugged.

"I say we try it once. If that doesn't work—that's it. We need to get out of here. Security could come back at any time."

Gina put a fingertip on the computer's touch screen. There was an immediately request for a password. She tapped the keyboard with ANNIES DOWN, all caps. A menu of files jumped onto the screen.

They stared at each other, Lolly's eyes bugged out.

Gina used the mouse to a link labeled: Caths. A spread sheet of numbers appeared. It looked confusing until she realized she was looking at a listing of various types of catherizations. Then she could see that the five-digit numbers following the procedures were all in the neighborhood of ten-thousand dollars.

"How many Caths does Tallent do on an average day?" she asked Lolly.

"Two to four, or at least that's the way it's been since I started working here."

"Wow! With only two days of procedures per week, that's close to a hundred and fifty grand a month."

They heard the whistling again. This time it was the Beatle's *Yesterday* getting louder and louder. From the way the light bounced, Gina could tell it was coming from the other direction this time.

"Damn!" Gina closed the files and a caduceus popped back on the screen.

They dropped to their knees and huddled together again.

The computer monitor was still glowing brightly—it had yet to go into sleep mode. With the whistling almost on top of Tallent's office, Gina quickly stood and pushed the button to turn off the monitor screen, then dropped back down a second or two before the watchman's flashlight beam went from wall to wall in the office.

Gina was ready to throw up from the bile burning the back of her throat. Lolly was squeezing her arm as though she was trying to strangle it.

The guard continued on his way, but he stopped whistling for a long moment, and then continued on. *Yesterday* came trilling out.

They waited five minutes, according to Gina's illuminated watch dial, before retracing the steps they'd taken up to the office. Gina crossed her fingers as they stepped silently down the stairs to the first floor, then hurried out the front door.

When Lolly pulled out her car keys, a frantic look crossed her face.

"My ID tag is gone. It must have fallen out of my pocket."

"Oh, shit!"

* * *

When Gina walked into the apartment, Harry was sitting on the sofa, facing the door. "Where have you been? I tried calling you but it went to message."

She sat down next to him, rested her head on his shoulder. "Don't be angry. I went with Lolly to Tallent's office."

"Gina!" Harry clutched her arm.

"Lolly was going to go alone. I couldn't let her do that. I was afraid for her."

"And now I'm afraid for you."

Chapter 18

Gina and Harry were right on time the next morning, moving smoothly through traffic on their way to Ridgewood Hospital. The Fiat was behaving the way she was supposed to—no hiccups, no coughs, no indigestion. She sounded like she was in perfect health.

"You know, Harry, I feel so guilty for not telling Mulzini about my suspicions. You know, about Mort Tallent. But I can't help it—it just goes against the grain to erode someone's confidence in their doctor."

"What could you say, doll? Hey Mulzini, don't see that doc—he might be behind a couple of murders."

"That man can be such a pain in the ass sometimes. He had an A-1 referral to Robert Cantor, but no, he would have had to wait to get an appointment."

"Yeah," Harry said, "waiting's not exactly Mulzini's style. Guess he wanted to get it over as soon as possible."

"I can understand that. But, he's going to Tallent! The man might be a crook, or a killer. I should have said something, or at least hinted at it."

"Still time to call him."

Gina found a parking place two blocks from the hospital.

"Well, how did I luck out like that?"

"Stick with me, babe—everything is coming up roses." Harry licked the tip of her fingers, then looked up and smiled at her.

Gina leaned over and kissed him on the nose, pulled out her phone, and tapped in Mulzini's home number. Marcia picked up on the first ring.

"Hi, Marcia. It's Gina Mazzio. You remember me?"

"Who can forget the bombshell nurse from the Bronx?" She laughed. "How are you?"

"I'm good. I wonder if I could speak to your husband?"

"Sure," Marcia said. "But he has a doctor's appointment at ten and the man's a nervous wreck."

Gina shifted in her seat. "Well, it's not important. Please tell him I was thinking of him and I expect a full report."

"You know Mulzini." Marcia laughed. "He'll tell you what he wants you to know—that's about the best you can hope for."

And then she was gone.

Gina dropped the cell back into her purse. Harry's eyes searched hers.

"I'm too late."

* * *

Mort Tallent sauntered into his office, as he did every work day—then stopped. There was an unfamiliar scent in the room; his dark plush carpet had a double trail of fresh footprints crossing over to his desk. He followed the impressions to his computer. Whoever had been here had come after the cleaning crew vacuumed at 10 p.m.

He sat down and stared at the monitor. His secret recorder showed no unauthorized security breaches.

He opened the desk drawer. Everything was as he'd left it, except for his *Time Out* health club membership card—it was turned over to reveal his password, ANNIE'S DOWN. Someone had been here, used his password, and gone through his computer files.

He picked up the phone for his receptionist. "Maya, please come into my office."

It was barely a moment before she stood at his doorway. "Yes, Doctor?"

"Get hold of the head of building security. Tell him I need to see him in my office.

Right now!"

"Yes, Doctor."

While she was gone, he searched every drawer and found nothing suspicious. Of course, there really wasn't anything in his desk to be worried about. That wasn't the problem—it was his computer.

He felt sick.

I take care of one problem and another one pops up like a noxious weed.

Maria was out of the picture—who could have been here poking around?

He forced himself back into his routine and brought up his schedule for today's patients. They were all consults except for a four p.m. surgery—someone too important and too busy to fit into Tallent's normal scheduling.

Someone who doesn't realize how weak and fragile the human body is. Someone who thinks he's still in control even when he's decked out, drugged out, and on a surgical table. Someone very stupid.

He was putting on a fresh white coat when Maya brought a bouncer-type person to the door of his office—tall, muscled, rough-looking, but neatly dressed in a business suit.

"This is Jerry, Doctor Tallent." Maya said.

"Come in, Jerry. Just a few questions."

"Good morning, sir."

"What time did the janitors leave the building last night?"

Jerry looked at an eight-and-a-half by eleven clipboard, turned over a couple of pages, and said, "That would be twelve a.m., sir, according to the time clock. "

"Did any of your security guards report anything unusual."

Jerry checked his notes again. "No, sir. Well, except for a lost identification card—one of employees in your department. I was going to return it to her today."

"No need," Tallent said, holding out his hand. "I'll do it for you. Thanks."

The head of security removed the ID card from his clipboard and gave it to Tallent.

"Before you go, Jerry, do you have the security tapes from last night?"

"Sure. We always keep them for at least forty-eight hours."

Tallent nodded. "Great! How long will it take for you to make a copy and bring it to me?

Jerry smiled. "I'll have it for you in fifteen minutes."

"Perfect."

* * *

Tallent plugged in the flash drive Jerry had delivered to Maya for him. He sat back in his chair and watched. He'd never seen the tapes that the single camera took throughout the day.

He sped through the video. He could see himself coming and going, Maya popping into his office on and off throughout the day. Every patient he saw had ended up as part of this digitized record. There was also a lot of back-and-forth of personnel, as well as Cantor and Brichett popping in to talk. Later the janitors with their cleaning gear entered his office— then the motion-sensitive surveillance camera went into sleep mode.

He was bored and about to extract the flash drive when the camera awakened and went back into action. He sat upright in his chair. At first there were only shadows, then Lolly Stentz was walking down the hall in front of someone. Lolly looked scared to death. In a moment another face that he knew from the Ridgewood CCU entered the frame.

"Gotcha! Gotcha both!"

Chapter 19

Mulzini was sitting on the end of the bed in his underwear, trying hard to push himself up to finish dressing. He had a ten a.m. appointment with Dr. Morton Tallent.

Man, I don't want to go.

The thought no sooner disappeared than his neck started hurting and with that came shortness of breath.

I gotta go, gotta find out what's going on with this damn aging body of mine. Life has turned me into a broken-down, fifty-year-old. When did that happen?

He stood, pulled slacks and a sport shirt out of the closet, threw them on a chair. Marcia stuck her head in the doorway. "Not ready, yet?"

"No, I'm just trying to get myself into gear. I'm getting there."

"Okay, but we don't want to be late."

"There is no we," Mulzini growled at her. "You're not going with me."

"Oh, yeah? Think again, big guy. I'll be right there with you—and I think you already knew that."

He smiled. "Yeah, yeah."

"Oh, by the way, Gina called."

"What's up?"

"She just wanted to wish you well."

"Does the whole world know about my appointment? Oh, yeah—wait a minute; I guess I told her about it."

"Get with it, man." Then Marcia was gone.

He'd barely got one arm into his shirt sleeve when Dirk walked into the room. Without a word he walked up to Mulzini and threw his arms around him and hugged him, then held onto his arm. He wouldn't let go. "You're going to be fine, Pops."

Mulzini looked at the earnest face so full of life and hope—so unlike the kid he'd found homeless in Golden Gate Park a year ago. Marcia fell in love with Dirk instantly and so did Mulzini. He'd never regretted bringing the boy home and into their lives.

"Yeah, yeah." Mulzini had to turn his head away when tears started filling his eyes.

"I know you're scared," Dirk said.

"Hey, bite your tongue you little brat."

"A brat, maybe, but I'm turning seventeen in a few months—not so little anymore." He pulled Mulzini back into his arms and they both spontaneously started crying on each other's shoulder.

Mulzini stepped back. "You better not ever tell Marcia about this."

"About what?" Dirk pulled a handkerchief out of his pocket, gave it to Mulzini then took it back and mopped his own face. "Good luck today. I'll see you later."

"Need some bucks?" Mulzini said pulling a twenty out of his wallet.

"Naw. Hauling furniture on weekends keeps me rolling in the stuff."

They both laughed and Dirk was out the door.

* * *

After checking in with the receptionist, Mulzini and Marcia sat down in the waiting area of cardiologists. Mulzini reached over and squeezed her hand. "If anything happens to me, you need to know most of my important papers are in the top right-hand drawer of my desk."

"Will you stop that?" she said. "It's only an office visit. We're here to get information. Hell, you're a cop, you should know what that's all about."

"Marcia, I know something bad is going to happen. I just feel it." His heart was racing and he could barely sit still.

"Now you stop it, right now, Stephano Mulzini."

"You know better than to call me that name."

"Oh, I know you hate it. But it's my way of throwing cold water in your face." She leaned across the arms of the two leather chairs and kissed him on the lips. "You're here for help—not to die. Try to remember that, please."

The door to the office area opened. A slender woman came into the room and looked around. The other four people sitting in the room looked up from whatever they were doing. Mulzini assumed, from their expressions, that not one of them wanted to be next. He knew he didn't.

"Mr. and Mrs. Mulzini?"

Only the first of many unwanted questions.

They both nodded.

"My name is Maya. Allow me to take you in to see the doctor."

They stood and followed the chic woman down the hallway. She paused at one of the doors, opened it, led them inside, and showed them to a pair of matching walnut and leather chairs placed in front of a large desk.

"The doctor will be with you in a moment or two," Maya said and left the room.

Mulzini barely had time to give the office a quick once-over when a tall, fiftyish man came in and stood before them.

"Mr. and Ms. Mulzini, I'm Dr. Tallent." He reached out and shook both their hands.

Mulzini could tell just from his handshake that this man didn't like to touch people. His whole body language didn't inspire any sort of confidence. There was something off about him. Tallent sat down behind his desk.

"I see from the form you filled out that you work for the police department?"

Another question.

"Is that some kind of problem?" Mulzini said. Marcia squeezed his arm as if to say, "Cool it!"

Tallent gave him a phony chuckle. "No, no, of course not. It's just that that must be a very stressful job."

"It has its moments." Mulzini felt as though he already had this man's probing fingers wandering up and down his body. "I deal with it."

Tallent nodded. "I see from your internist's notes that you refused to get any of the tests he ordered."

Mulzini could feel the hairs on his neck getting prickly, a warning that he was about to lose his temper. He took a couple of deep breaths and calmed himself. "Look, my doc already talked to me about atrial fib until it was coming out of my eyeballs. I had all those tests a year ago, when this AF crap started."

Marcia dug her nails into his arm, letting him know he was getting out of line.

Dr. Tallent's face flushed. "Look, Stefano—"

"—do not call me that!"

"I don't understand—isn't that your name?"

"My name is Mulzini. That's what I like to be called—please."

"Okay, sir. Your internist found that you had no structural damage to your heart, however, no one has examined your blood vessels to see if there are any other problems that might be causing you ..." He paused and ran one finger down a sheet of paper in front of him. "Let me see—shortness of breath, fatigue, and, of course, your episodes of increased AF."

"They recommended a cath a year ago, but he refused," Marcia said.

Mulzini glared at her, then turned back to Tallent. "Maybe I didn't have the cath, but I'm not going through that whole business again. I don't want to take all of those tests a second time, understand?"

"Well, sir, I see you've had a twenty-four-hour AF episode and they had to do a cardio-version to set you back to a normal rhythm."

"Yeah, yeah, I hear you. Next thing up is the stroke business."

"And the fact you refused to take the anti-clotting medicine," Marcia said.

"Look, doc. I'm in a risky profession. I can't afford to be on anything where I can keep bleeding. A cut can do that to you, right?"

Tallent threw his notes on his desk and ignored the question. "Look, Mr. Mulzini, we can set you up for the Cath Lab right here in our offices."

"No hospital?"

"No. We have our own CCU right here. There's a good chance an ablation might be the answer for you."

"Yeah, my internist discussed that."

"You might also have narrowing of an artery—"

"Look, I know all that crap. Just set me up so I can get back to my life."

"Okay, sir. Let's get to your physical and we'll go from there."

Chapter 20

Cal's arms were wrapped around her. He tongued her neck, trailing downward over her breasts, her belly. They were sucking up each other's breath while his hands rode her hips, her bottom—lifting her onto his cock ... writhing, moving faster, frantic ... gulping for air, drowning in each other ... screaming with joy.

Kat Parker jolted back to reality. She was having one of those daydreams again. She'd been doing that a lot lately. The kind of mind games or fantasies you know aren't real, but feel real and urgent. She snapped out of it, looked around. But she was safe in her office.

She wished she could stop thinking about Cal Cortez. She hardly knew him; he'd only come into her life two days ago, almost right after she went to see Dr. Tallent.

She shouldn't have even met him, but she'd filled in for someone who was out sick—she'd had to finalize his employment entry into Golden Eye Tech.

The minute he walked in the door she was caught. He was not only handsome, in a rugged kind of way, he was an anomaly in her world. It was rare she met any employee over fifty. Technology was filled with thirty and forty-year-olds, at least the ones she'd met.

"My name is Cal Cortez," he'd said with a nervous laugh. "But you already know that."

"Yes." Then they just sat looking at each other; it wasn't at all uncomfortable or disquieting. It was pure attraction, something she'd forgotten about along the way.

"Are you free for dinner?' He'd blurted it out.

Before that, she was lost and lonely, but one day, one moment had changed it all.

Something real happened to her that day.

Kat had not felt well for so long that it was surprising that since she met Cal and saw Dr. Tallent, things had gotten so much better. Maybe her life would now change for the better.

Was it meeting someone new and vital? Was it because she was finally going to do something positive about her health—have the cardiac catheterization and find out once and for all what was the matter with her, if anything?

Dr. Tallent tried to explain the procedure, had gone over the possible disastrous things that could happen, even though he'd made it plain that having a stroke or developing a blood clot was statistically very low. It all seemed unimportant compared with all the benefits she would get from just knowing about her physical situation.

She started daydreaming again and right on cue, her phone rang. It was Cal.

"Hi, Kat."

"Hi." She was totally breathless thinking about his green eyes and they way they seemed to swallow her.

"How about I make us dinner at my apartment tonight?"

It caught her totally off guard. "I ... I'd love to."

"I'll come and get you at five. Okay?"

"Yes. I'm looking forward to it."

The minute she hung up she tried to remember what underwear she'd worn, not that they'd necessarily become intimate, even though she knew they both wanted to. At least, she did.

Now she was restless and when she tried to pick up where she'd left off on a project sitting on her computer screen, she couldn't remember what was so important about it. Instead, she started daydreaming again.

* * *

Tallent picked up his phone. "Maya, please bring Lolly Stentz in to see me right away."

"Yes, doctor."

He sat at his desk flipping Lolly's employee card over and over. The metallic strip on the back served as a key that allowed her entry into every section of the penthouse offices. This one little key could be the beginning of the end. If it wasn't so serious, it would be amusing.

Done in by a stupid little nothing.

"Hi, Mort. You wanted to see me?"

Even though he expected her, her voice startled him. She stood at the doorway—had on her soft head cap, scrubs, and shoe coverings.

"Come in, Lolly. Close the door, please." He could tell she was nervous—her body was tense and she was slightly bent as she approached his desk and slid into the leather chair opposite him.

He leaned back, tapped a pen from point to top, back and forth, drawing the moment out. She shifted in her seat, apparently trying to get comfortable.

"What were you doing in my office last night?"

She looked stunned, but blurted, "Why?"

"Why?" he said, trying to hold back a sneer. "Because you don't belong in here."

"How—"

—Tallent pointed to her employee ID card on the desk in front of him, flipped it over, and tapped it as if it was a winning blackjack card.

"You know, I was wondering what happened to my card. I thought I'd lost it in the employee parking garage." She gave him a tentative smile.

"I think you lost it when you and Gina Mazzio were here last night." He leaned forward, half-way across the desk. "We have you on our security tapes—don't try to deny it."

She leaned back into the seat and laughed. "I should have known." She grabbed a tissue from her pocket and blew her nose. "You know Gina Mazzio—she works in CCU at Ridgewood."

"Of course I know her. She's also the one who recommended you to Robert for this job."

"Well, she was curious about the offices and our own little CCU set up so I brought her here after hours to show her around."

"It was after three in the morning, Lolly."

"I know it was dumb, but when we're all busy it's hard to show off the place."

"And you were in my office and at my computer. Is that part of the tour?"

"I don't know why we did that," she laughed nervously. "Sort of when the cat's

away, the mouse will play kind of thing." She held up a hand. "I know, pretty lame. But she was curious." She shifted in her seat again.

"Enough to go through my desk drawers?"

"I'm sorry. I admit it was pretty dumb, but we both suffer from insomnia and it seemed like a fun thing to do. I hope you'll forgive my stupidity. "

He held her eyes for a long moment. "Go on, get out of here—go do your job."

She was up like a shot. "Please forgive me."

He nodded at her.

Not a chance in hell, you lying piece of shit.

* * *

Lolly left Mort Tallent's office, hurried to the bathroom, and locked herself in. She looked in the mirror.

She was white as chalk. The face staring back at her was one of a scared-shitless human being—her eyes were watery and when she removed her surgical cap, her hair was soaking wet and plastered to her head.

Did Tallent believe me?

Not for a minute!

Maria was dead, along with her mother, for interfering in Tallent's affairs. That was it, plain and simple. Was she next? Was Gina?

She washed her face with cold water and patted it dry with paper towels, tried to puff up her hair—she would have to get a fresh cap. And looking at the sweat stains mapping under her arms meant she needed to change into fresh scrubs as well.

Lolly pulled out her phone and tapped in Gina's number, hoping she would be in a spot where she could grab her phone to talk.

Gina picked up right away. "Lolly? Are you all right. Is there anything the matter?"

"I just spent the most uncomfortable ten minutes of my life."

"What happened."

"Tallent is on to us."

"What do you mean, Lolly. How could he be?"

"Well, remember when I dropped my employee card?"

"Oh!"

"He returned it to me. Not only that—he reviewed their security tapes and saw both you and me sneaking through the place."

"Oh, my God! This is awful. Is he going to fire you?"

"I don't think so. But, I know he didn't believe a word I said."

* * *

Gina met Harry in the cafeteria for their lunch break. Her eyes were a big as saucers as she told him about Tallent, how he knew she and Lolly had been in his office.

All kinds of scenarios flashed through his head.

"This is just what I was afraid of, Gina."

"If you say, I-told-you-so, I swear I'll scream."

"Look, doll, this is how you always get in over your head." Harry grabbed her hand, squeezed it. "Now you're not only in the middle of a murder case, you could be charged with breaking into Tallent's office."

Gina covered her face. "He wouldn't call the police, would he?"

"Actually, I don't know why he hasn't done it already."

She thought a moment. "I'll tell you why: because he's involved with Maria's murder. He's not going to run to the police and chance their radar picking up his signals."

"Maybe."

"Lolly is not one to push the panic button about anything, but she was worried about the bookkeeper, and then Maria she was dead, along with her mother."

"You have to forgive me, doll." Harry moved his chair closer to her. "I'm selfish, I know, but this was supposed to be our time ... like getting into wedding plans, doing something that was fun instead of always getting into the middle of some life or death crisis."

She looked at him and her eyes filled with tears. "It's what I want, too. But I can't turn my back on a friend. You wouldn't do that either."

Harry nodded. "You're probably right, besides, it's too late." Harry leaned over and kissed her cheek. "You've gotten yourself smack in the middle now."

Chapter 21

Mulzini and Marcia took the elevator down from the penthouse offices of the cardiologists. Neither of them said a word. Marcia reached for Mulzini's hand and he felt safe for the moment.

Outside, he pulled her along with him. Crowds were wandering back and forth and there was an energy that revved him up. Almost as good as being at the Indy 500.

"The car's the other way," Marcia said, smiling up at him.

"Yeah, but I like being around these San Francisco people. They make me feel feisty. Like I'm still here kicking."

"Not feeling sorry for yourself, are you?" Marcia tugged at his arm. "Are you?"

"Naw, we've all gotta go sometime. Maybe this is my time."

"Time, schmime! You listen to me, big guy: don't you even think about checking out, you hear? You're here with me, and that's the way it's going to be."

She stopped, pulled his head down to her, and kissed his cheek. Crowds moved around them, but he could see people were looking at them and smiling.

"Hey, see that lunch cart? Let's get a couple of dogs. I'm actually hungry."

"If it's junk food, you're *always* hungry." She laughed and lightly punched his arm.

"Hot dogs aren't junk food—they're basic to human nutrition. How do you think I've lasted this long?"

After slathering their dogs with mustard, onions, and relish, they moved back away from the cart and started eating.

"So, are you up for doing the cardiac cath next week?" Marcia said.

"Wow, it's that soon?"

Marcia nodded as she finished chewing the last bite of the impromptu lunch. "At least it's going to be at Ridgewood. Gina will keep me in the loop."

"Yeah. I gotta get it over with so I can get back to work. That way I'll stop driving both of us nuts."

"And, Dirk, too. He looked like he'd been crying after talking with you this morning. What was that about?"

"Nothing really." Mulzini stuffed the rest of the hot dog into his mouth. Talked around it. "He was just reassuring me, while I reassured him. That kid's a treasure."

"Yeah, one of the few perks you've brought home from the job."

* * *

Mort Tallent sat in his BMW outside the Time Out Health Club.

He'd bought a pack of cigarettes and started smoking again—something he hadn't done in almost fifteen years. While he inhaled the tobacco smoke, he hoped it would calm his nerves, help him think. But he realized that all the smoking did was push him back into a deadly habit.

This morning, after talking to Lolly, he'd hurried through his consultations so he could get out for an early lunch. He wasn't interested in food. He wanted a resolution.

He sat there and devised a plan for handling everything, thought about again bringing Vlad into the messy equation. The Russian was unpredictable, violent, unstable, and, worst of all, already had too much incriminating information on Tallent. But did he have a choice?

He was worried, though. If he went ahead and had Vlad take care of Lolly for him, it would be much too soon after the murders of Maria and her mother.

And since Maria had worked in his office, some nosy cop might drag up the connection between that and the death of his ex-wife, Annie. Too many deaths involving the office of Dr. Morton Tallent?

His head was exploding.

For the millionth time he cursed his dead ex-wife for causing him to get involved with the hit man.

It was getting too messy—all fingers could soon be pointing at Mort Tallent.

Not only that, Lolly had brought in her friend Gina Mazzio. Another CCU medical tie in.

He lit another cigarette with the old stub.

No, he would have to wait it out. See how the cards fell. There was no doubt that Vlad was definitely needed, but getting *rid* of Lolly wasn't the answer. There were other ways.

He took a couple of deep breaths, put out the freshly lit cigarette.

Chapter 22

The man leaned against a store front on the corner, cell in hand. He was looking at the phone window, like every other person around him, as though there was something there that mattered.

What he was really doing was looking across the street at Vlad Folo walking up the steps into the Time Out Health Club.

He was profiling Vlad—age , height, weight, physical condition. Even at this distance it wasn't difficult to read Vlad's body language—confidence. The man tapped into the stored notes in his smart phone, data he'd been carrying with him for a long time. This might or might not be the person he was looking for, but all of the superficial details seemed to fit.

He waited a few minutes, crossed the street, and walked into the club. A very attractive receptionist looked up from her desk and smiled at him.

"May I help you?"

"Yes, I do believe you can." He gave her a bright smile and leaned over her desk.

* * *

Vlad was feeling particularly good this morning. Instead of his usual raw egg and twelve- ounces of orange juice, consumed in his kitchen, he'd gone out to eat a large breakfast of pancakes swimming in maple syrup, along with four sausage links, all topped off with an extravagant four cups of black coffee.

Every bite warned that he would have to pay a physical price to compensate for all that food. He knew it was going to take more than one heavy-duty, two-hour workout to make it all right again.

At the club, he winked at the receptionist, who was still trying to get him into bed, and then walked through the facility, past the squash rooms, the pool, the spa, and the steam rooms.

When he finally got to his locker, he shucked off his expensive sport coat and sharply-creased wool pants, and pulled down his underwear, leaving him stark naked.

The locker room was empty, not that it would have mattered, but he turned to a full-length mirror and studied his body as he flexed his muscles. His eyes traveled downward and he stared at his penis. It was long and very healthy.

And very active.

Yes, he was beautiful to look at. That's what both women and men said about him.

When he lived on the streets, men would seek him out, beg him to suck them off, take it, or give it in the ass, and they always paid with very large bills if they wanted to see him again.

They always did want to see him again.

Those funds could have paid for a small apartment, but he continued to sleep in the alleys or gang members' pads. He changed where he settled down from week to week and it served him well, especially after he became a hit man for a gang. He not only protected, he was well protected, too.

His father's warning to stay low, blend in, never left his thoughts. Papa also warned that he would never escape from the Russian killers, no matter how smart, or how much he tried. But Vlad was now thirty two and knew his lessons in survival had served him well.

His father was wrong.

It had all been hard, but he'd escaped.

Vlad reached into his locker and grabbed workout shorts and sneakers. He put them on and walked out to the large exercise room where a large array of machines and weights were waiting.

Idle chatter drifted into silenced as he walked into the gym. He nodded to various people, mostly body trainers and clients.

He knew how beautiful he was and so did they.

Chapter 23

After Tallent waved goodbye on his way out to lunch, Robert Cantor was immediately up and down the hall. He walked in on Jon Brichett, who was on the phone and gave Cantor a wait-a-minute hand signal.

When Brichett hung up, he said, "Those post-op call-backs can be a bitch." He shook his head. "Bring them in or nurse them along at home and worry about them the whole time." He shook his head. "Don't ask me why I became a doctor."

His partner remained silent.

"So, Bob, what's up? You've got that pissed-off look plastered all over your face."

Cantor didn't quite know how to structure his concern about Mort Tallent and the strange way he was behaving. He finally said, "Have you noticed anything unusual or different about Mort's behavior lately?"

Jon Brichett was the youngest of the three partners, and generally had an upbeat personality. Cantor knew he was loved by everybody, especially his patients. His opinion would definitely help structure and solidify whatever Cantor was thinking.

"Now that you mention it, I have," Brichett said. "What's bothering the man?"

"What could it be?" Cantor said. "He makes twice as much money as we do, he's single, foot-loose, and fancy-free. Hell, I'd give anything for that kind of life."

"I'll tell you, Bob, that bachelor life looks a lot better from the outside looking in—much more exciting than it really is." He gave him a know-it-all smile, "Speaking theoretically, of course."

Cantor laughed. "Hey, that's for sure. I wouldn't give up my life with Stacy for anything." He collapsed into one of the chairs. "And being a bachelor certainly doesn't seem to make Mort too happy."

"I thought when that whole business with his ex quieted down he'd come out of that dark hole he's fallen into. I mean having the police questioning him about Annie's death really took its toll on him."

Cantor looked hard at Brichett. "I think Annie sleeping around absolutely destroyed Mort's whole world. He was crazy about her." Cantor hesitated. "There's more to Mort than you might think. Were you aware that his family, particularly his father, pushed him into medicine?"

"No, never heard anything about that."

"Back in the day, Mort was a competitive surfer. Loved it. Traveled everywhere for that one perfect big wave." Cantor shifted in his seat. "I saw a video of him competing once—he was awesome. But his family didn't see it that way. Pushed, and I mean *really* pushed, him into medicine. I met his mom & dad once."

"What were they like?"

Cantor chuckled. "Society-type snobs. Looked down on anyone not in their stratosphere—including me."

"Can't say that about Mort. He'd just as soon talk to the janitor as to me."

"I didn't really know anything about his background, just that he's a respected practitioner," Brichett said. "Actually, He's always been a little standoffish to me from the first time I met him. I didn't think he liked me, didn't think he'd agree to bring me into the practice."

"Naw, he liked you all right. It's that sunny disposition of yours. It's hard to take with a hangover."

Brichett gave him an evil glare. "Very funny."

"Besides, standoffish is one thing," Cantor said. "But he's just been plain off the wall since Annie died. That was over a year ago, and it's getting worse." He ran his fingers through what was left of his hair and realized he was doing that a lot, maybe to reassure himself that there was any left. "We probably should talk to him about taking some time off, getting his act together. Maybe that's all he needs."

Brichett sat up taller in his seat. "Are you kidding me? We can't take care of our patient load with the three of us."

"Well, let's think about it. At least talk to him." The pros and cons were lining up in Cantor's head. "Sometime soon."

* * *

Kat Parker was a nervous wreck all afternoon. All she could think about was Cal. She'd had so many fantasies about him, and yet, she barely knew him. Going home with him was slamming her with too much reality.

She was frightened. What if he looked at her, was turned off by her, by her body.

I should never have said yes to having dinner at his house. What a fool I am. I was secure out in public, secure in a restaurant with people all around us.

At four, she went into the rest room and reapplied her make-up and took a few minutes to try to meditate. Meditation was the only thing that had gotten her through her separation and divorce from her husband. For some unknowable, stupid reason she'd abruptly stopped the practice at home and tried to keep it up at work.

She'd sit on a toilet seat in the bathroom with the door securely locked. When she would drift into a meditative zone, someone would come into the room, start banging things around, generally making noise that would cut right into her concentration. She finally gave up. Starting again today wasn't going to help her.

Kat tried to get her thoughts together, but when five finally arrived, she didn't know what she'd done with the whole afternoon except worry and check herself every few minutes in the mirror.

At five-ten she was wasted and decided to leave. He must have changed his mind. She couldn't just sit here. She had to get away.

She grabbed her purse from the desk drawer, gathered her jacket, ready to leave. Cal came flying through the door to her office. She could tell he must have run across the entire Golden Eye campus, and his office was at the opposite end of the huge corporate grounds. Perspiration was dripping off of his face and he was breathless.

"Kat, I'm sorry. I couldn't get out of a last minute meeting." He stopped short and looked closely at her. "Did you think I wasn't coming?"

"I ... I didn't know."

Without a word he gathered her up in his arms, murmured, "I would never do that. Especially to you."

Her legs started to give way, but he held her up.

* * *

Cal made a wonderful pasta diner, but at first she thought she wouldn't be able to eat. Then the combination of food and wine, and just talking about themselves, made her relax and really dig in.

He lived in a small apartment on Valencia Street in a part of San Francisco that had recently become very trendy. Many in the tech industry, especially from their own company, had moved into the area, driving rentals sky high.

"Actually until I got the job at Golden Eye, I thought I was going to have to move out."

"How long have you lived here?"

"About five years. They've raised the rent three times since then."

Cal was playing an old time CD by Frank Sinatra. He stood, held out a hand to her—soon she was in his arms and they were dancing to "Witchcraft." She was floating from the wine, and she felt at home.

"I knew from the moment I saw you we would be like this," he said. "There was just something—"

"—don't say anything else ... I just want to be into the moment, be here with you."

Cal leaned into her and they melded together, kissing until she was breathless. She tugged at his shirt; his hands rode her hips, slid over her body until she couldn't stop herself. She had to touch him all over.

"Stay with me tonight, please."

"Oh, yes," she murmured.

Chapter 24

After Tallent interrogated Lolly in his office, she'd been jumpy and sick with fear the rest of the day. Why hadn't she thought about the security tapes? Today, everyone used them. And of course, they would pick up the two of them wandering through the penthouse after hours. How stupid could she be?

And we never even got the information we went after. Shit! What was it that Maria had seen?

Lolly was scared, but she was also stubborn. She couldn't stop thinking about the other doctors' computers. Maybe the same billing information would be available there and she could pick up on whatever it was the bookkeeper had seen.

Nosing around the other employees, she discovered that each doctor had his own bookkeeper, kept separate books, and they all paid into one expense fund for maintaining the office. It seemed they were actually three separate practices sort of semi-merged into one business.

One of the other nurses got suspicious about all of her questioning. "Why are you so interested in their finances? We don't get into the financial part of their practice. What are you up to?"

"Just curious."

It was obvious that answer wasn't going to hold off her or anybody else. Lolly had to back off. She still wasn't going to let Tallent get away with the deaths of Maria and her mother. She knew Tallent had to be involved. Lolly vowed she would find the answers and would stop dragging Gina into the whole mess.

After questioning her in his office, Tallent stayed away from her, requesting other nurses' services throughout the day—she ended up working mostly with Bob Cantor and Jon Brichett in the OR.

Every time she saw Mort Tallent, she managed to find something else to do to stay out of his way. The last thing she wanted was any kind of face-to-face with him again—about anything.

She knew she wasn't off the hook for breaking into his office. He wasn't the forgive-and-forget kind of guy. He'd find a way to get back at her. It puzzled her that he didn't out and out fire her. That's what any other doctor would have done.

Lucky Gina—at least he held no power over her.

Power had occupied Lolly's career-staging with every job she took. She learned early on that hospital hierarchies were simply not designed in the nurses' favor. They had little clout in a doctor-hospital relationship that fed off of each other. Nurses were there as a service to the patients and doctors. Without unions they would have been powerless.

She was happy when the day was over; he was one of the last to leave the penthouse offices. When she stepped out of the elevator into the garage, she sensed something was off.

Gina talked about an eye-twitch being her antenna for trouble. For Lolly, it was her neck—like a dog, her muscles would bunch up as a warning. She took a careful look around, Saw nothing to feed her suspicions.

Nothing. Nothing here. You're just jumpy because of Tallent.

She picked up her pace, hurried to her car, dragging the key out of her purse as she walked. She was focused on clicking the electronic door opener when someone grabbed her around the neck. She tried to scream, but she couldn't speak, couldn't breathe. She was suffocating, fading into darkness.

* * *

Lolly was in a black hole. She could hear music off someplace in the distance and she drifted in that direction.

Her eyes snapped open.

Memories of choking and suffocating became stronger, and with that, all her senses started kicking into gear. The fear

106

of attack that every female in her old Bronx neighborhood knew well, struck her hard.

Someone had snatched her.

Her heart was clawing at her chest; she could hardly swallow with something wrapped tightly across her mouth. She turned her head and globs of drool dripped out from the corner of her mouth and ran down her naked chest and shoulder. She looked down.

She was completely stripped.

What was she doing naked in an empty room? Her breaths came in snorts and gasps. She wanted to scream, but all she could do was grunt.

She turned her head as far she could in every direction. The only furniture in the entire room appeared to be the bed she was lying on. Spread-eagled, arms and legs tied at the four corners of the bed. She twisted and tugged but there was no give in the bindings.

A voice startled her; floated out of nothingness. "I see you're finally awake."

A man came around from behind the headboard of the bed, walked up to her side, bent over, and licked her face.

He slowly ran a finger down from the top of her head, across her nose and mouth, through the space between her flattened breasts, onto her belly, and into to her bush. He plunged one finger deep inside of her.

Stopstopstopstopstopstop!

She wiggled furiously, jerked her hips up, tried to get away from him. But he was there no matter what she did.

His eyes, intense, never left hers. His gaze seemed to bore straight through her head.

"What were you and the other woman doing in the doctor's office?"

She grunted.

He laughed and uncovered her mouth. "So, you're still not going to say anything? He pulled the invading finger from her vagina, straightened to his full height, and moved out of sight behind the headboard.

Ohmygodohmygodohmygod. I'm going to die here. He's going to kill me.

When he came back, he was nude. Now she could see the massive shoulders, bulging muscles, and engorged penis that had been hidden beneath his clothing.

He held a stiletto in one hand. "Look at me! Take a long look. I'm beautiful, right?" His eyelids narrowed to slits.

She nodded, saw his eyes almost close and his lips pull back to reveal his teeth. She quickly nodded again, and again.

Gonna killmekillme.

In a single motion, he leaped onto the bed, straddled her, and held her tight with his knees. He raised the stiletto high above her. She watched the needle-sharp point of the knife come down ever so slowly until the tip touched her skin. He lifted one breast, caressed it, and laced the blade through it again and again.

She screamed. Sounds of a desperate, trapped animal filled the room.

At the peak of her shrieks, he jammed himself inside her and rode her like a cowboy, never letting up. Her mind started slipping away. Every thought, every feeling became a wave of pain, repeating itself until she escaped into unconsciousness.

When she woke again, she was stretched out on the back seat of her car, the stiletto still impaled in her breast. There was a damp note resting on her bare belly. She lifted it with trembling hands and wiped away tears so she could read it:

GO AWAY AND DON'T COME BACK
NEXT TIME YOU DIE

Chapter 25

Gina paced back and forth in the living room, then stopped at the window and stared at the deluge of rain. "I don't understand it, I'm really worried about Lolly. It's not like her."

"The message was on your phone?" Harry was flaked out on the sofa. He twisted around and sat up. "It does seem odd that she would leave a text message for that kind of thing. What did it say again?"

Gina reached for her cell and read: "I'm writing to you from the airport. Don't try to reach me. I'm going back home. California was a big mistake."

"Jeez. When did she leave you that message?"

"About eight."

"You'll never be able to reach her until tomorrow."

"There's more." She held the phone so he could see.

He read it out loud: "Protect yourself. Stay away from Tallent."

"Something must have happened to make her run like this." Gina plopped down next to him. "Probably something to do with getting nailed on those security tapes."

"I was afraid there'd be blow-back from that little adventure. " He took her hand.

"I don't know," she said. "Cooking the books is bad enough, but do you think Mort Tallent would really do something vicious to scare Lolly off."

"Well, hell, Gina, you and Lolly were accusing him of being involved in his bookkeeper's death. If he did have a hand in it, why wouldn't he do most *anything* to get clear?"

"It's hard for me to think of doctors as killers—at least outside of their practice." She gave him a cynical smile. "Imagine going through all that schooling and training to save lives and then turn around and murder someone. It doesn't make sense to me."

Harry stood, went into the kitchen, came back with a bottle of wine and two glasses. "People change. Life and circumstances change all of us." He poured wine into each of the glasses.

"But murder?" Gina sipped at the wine. "What the hell can be in those books that's so devastating?"

"Tax evasions. Something illegal." Harry set his glass back on the coffee table after taking a sip, turned back to Gina, and took her hand. "Look, babe, he has you on tape breaking and entering—"

"—we didn't break in. Lolly had her employee card; we just walked in."

"Just a technicality. You were where you didn't belong."

"I suppose," Gina said

"That, as I've said before, could cause you real problems."

"All of this started with those accounting books. Maria and her mother are dead, and not only that, I heard from the hospital grapevine that Mort Tallent's ex-wife was also murdered. That's three deaths circling around the doctor's head." Gina grabbed onto his arm. "You don't think there's a connection do you? I mean, really?"

"I don't know, babe."

"Well, it's got my eyebrow twitching. Something's wrong. I can feel it."

Harry pulled her into his arms. "Can't you just let it go ... for us? We're getting married soon—Vinnie and Helen are getting married. Can't we just be light-hearted for a change?"

"I want to. I really do. But people are dead and my friend, Lolly, is gone because something to do with Tallent is dangerous and scary. It has to start with those books—I've got to get into them."

"You're not getting anywhere near his computer," Harry said. "I can tell you that."

"You're probably right. Maybe what we need is a hacker, someone who can get the job done."

Harry nodded.

"Do you know anyone like that?"

"You mean someone who's willing to risk going to jail because *you* ask for a favor."

"I guess so."

Harry looked long and hard at her. "Let it go, doll."

"I want to." She scratched her head for several seconds. "I promise I'll try."

Harry held her at arms' length. "But it's not going to happen, is it?"

She tried to smile but couldn't."

"Let me think about it. I might, I just *might* know someone."

Harry put his head on her shoulder. "Gina, on and off, during the last four years you have jumped from one nightmare to another. The thought of someone hurting you again—" he pulled her to him—"is more than I can stand."

* * *

The man sat in the rented BMW waiting. He'd watched Vlad Folo slip through the front door of the building—he looked at his watch—twenty minutes ago.

He was a patient man. He would sit there for as long as it took.

After another thirty minutes, Vlad came out and went to his black Cadillac, and slipped into the driver's seat.

The man noticed Vlad was dressed in a black running jacket and pants outfit. His body movements were that of a well-trained athlete. Even in the dim light of the street lamp, the man could see Vlad Folo moved like a panther on the hunt.

* * *

Mort Tallent sat in his high-rise condo and looked at the lights spread across the city. If he squinted, it became a mass of stars staring back at him. It reminded him of when he was a child. He would make everything a blur, because it always made life so much more beautiful—like a wonderful impressionist painting.

That's the way the world should be—never have to look, to study the details of anything. Once you do, it all turns ugly.

It reminded him of his dead ex-wife. Until he really got to know her, she was so beautiful. Like when they first met. She was young and as idealistic as he was. Surfing together, they were going to make the world a better place.

How dumb we were.

Surfing in the ocean, he felt connected—at one with everything that was or would ever be.

Lazy me. Didn't want to have to worry about money and survival. Just wanted to surf.

If he'd been brave he would have walked away from his parents and their insistence that he become a doctor. Just take Annie and run. He could have told them to take their money and shove it.

Instead, Annie got to go to school, he got to go to school, and neither got what they really wanted.

She'd been so, so perfect ... until she wasn't.

Even now, the thought of her being dead would catch him off guard and overwhelm him.

I made it happen.

He closed his eyes and began to cry. Soon he was sobbing so hard he didn't hear the doorbell at first. Then there was someone pounding at his door.

Mort jumped up, pulled a handkerchief from his pocket. "Just a minute." Dabbing at his eyes, he hurried to the door. "All right. Cut it out!"

He looked through the peep hole and there stood Vlad Folo, impatience written all over his face. Before he could release the deadbolt, Folo shouted at the door,

"Well, are you going to let me in or do I have to pick the lock, then come in there, and punch you in the face?"

Tallent pulled open the door and stepped aside. Folo brushed past him, went straight to the sofa, and made himself comfortable.

"That's better!" Folo said.

"How many times have I told you to never come to my place—either here or the office?"

"Damn, Doc, don't think I ever made a count. Besides, what makes you think I give a shit what you say?" He reached for one of the candies in a cut-crystal dish on the coffee table.. He carefully unwrapped the clear paper from a butterscotch sucker.

Tallent sat down in a chair opposite him, his stomach a roaring volcano. "What do you want?"

Vlad laughed. "What do I want? No, Mort, it's all about what you want." He sucked loudly on the candy. "Isn't that what we're all about?"

"Why are you here?"

"Lolly Stentz is now your ex-employee."

"You killed her?"

"No. You didn't want me to kill her, you cheap skate."

"What do you mean?"

"I mean you were too cheap to pay my fifty-thousand fee. That's what I mean."

Tallent was on the edge of his seat. "How did you get her to leave?"

"I simply advised her to go. She saw the reality of what her staying might lead to, so she left." He reached over for another sucker. This time a red one. "Right now, I believe she's taking an airplane ride back to wherever she came from."

"Did you hurt her?" Tallent jumped up.

"Sit down, Dr. Mort." He unwrapped the second candy and popped it into his mouth. "Of course I hurt her. Do you think she would have left any other way?"

113

Tallent slowly sat down again. "What do you want?"

"Well, first I want you to pay me the twenty-five thousand you owe me for Ms. Lolly. Then I want to know what you want done with the other one."

"The other one? You mean Gina Mazzio?"

Chapter 26

The minute Gina stepped onto the unit, Gwen, the team leader, was waiting for her. "Don't freak out, but I'm going to need you to scrub in for a Cardio Cath this morning."

"Oh, no, not yet, Gwen. I've hardly had any training for it. It'll be a mess."

"Believe me, it's not something that was planned." Gwen looked at her with sympathy. "But with two out sick, you're up." Gwen squeezed her arm. "Hey, you're gonna be fine."

"Who's the doctor doing it?"

"Mort Tallent." The team leader turned away as soon as she dropped the name on her. "Look, I know he's a pain," she said over her shoulder, "but we have to make it work. Keep your thoughts on the patient instead of him."

"I'll try."

"By the way, a friend of yours has signed up for a cath procedure. He named you as a go-to-person if there are any problems. You and his wife."

"Who is it?

Gwen opened her iPad and tapped on the screen. "Stefano Mulzini."

"Did you say Stefano?"

"Yes, that's right," Gwen said, checking her screen again.

"Well, thanks, Gwen." Gina s laughed for the first time since she arrived at work. "You'll never know how much that tidbit of information means to me."

* * *

Mort Tallent hadn't slept most of the night thinking about Vlad Folo and his unwelcome visit to his condo.

The man's a killer and he's getting more and more uncontrollable.

And why not. He has me by the balls. I'll never get him off my back now.

At that moment, he couldn't comprehend the madness that had caused him to contract Vlad to kill his ex-wife. Still, just thinking about Annie had him clenching his fists, fighting against anger that might flash or break loose at any moment. Worse, he knew he would feel like this for hours.

Of all the days that he didn't want to work at Ridgewood, this certainly topped the list. He had a violent headache and he was tired and worn down. If he could have been in his own Cath Lab, worked out of the penthouse, he would have been on safe territory.

Pull yourself together, Tallent.

He was scheduled for a cardiac cath, with a probable stent placement; all he wanted to do was crawl back into bed and sleep.

Tallent took the elevator to the Ridgewood CCU wing and was further irritated that construction workers were still at it in the hallway that joined the wing to the main hospital. He didn't like being in that dusty section. It kicked up his allergies.

When he walked into the actual unit, he went straight into the locker room and started to undress, hanging everything neatly in his locker. There were a couple of other doctors in the area, also getting into scrubs, but they did nothing more than exchange nods with Tallent.

Once he was ready, he checked his watch and saw he had enough time for a cup of coffee. He went into the staff lounge, headed straight for the coffee machine, and poured black coffee into a mug.

He eyed the staffing schedule and immediately saw Gina Mazzio next to his name. She would be his scrub nurse for the procedure.

* * *

Gina was setting up for the cardiac cath, trying not to think about the confrontation with Mort Tallent that was bound to happen.

What could she say when he asked why she was roaming through his offices after hours?

She tried to push it out of her mind as she continued with her set-up, went through her check list for the sterile field:

Sheaths, diagnostic caths, guide caths, guide wires.

Tallent's notes indicated this patient probably had severe narrowing of her arteries. She checked out the stents he might need, along with the angioplasty balloons.

She was feeling very insecure—she'd never scrubbed in for the procedure without a preceptor to guide her through the process. But the worse part, Tallent was known to give nurses a really bad time. He'd have more than enough opportunity, and reason, to really lay into her.

She waited, ready in her OR garb, sterile gloves on, fingers of both hands interlaced at chest level. She could see Tallent through the glass in the scrub area. He'd glanced at her a couple of times and his face above the mask appeared stern and hard.

Standing there, she had blocked out Gwen, who was working with the patient before the procedure began, but now she tuned into them again.

They were past the preliminary part, reiterating what meds the patient took and any known allergies. Gwen was at the point of giving the patient meds to help her relax and again going over what she could expect.

Their voices drifted away and she turned back to Tallent, who was almost finished with his scrub and ready to come into the OR. The circulating nurse lifted the covering sheet from the table setup, exposing all the instruments in the sterile field.

This could be the last day I work at Ridgewood.

Tallent stepped into the room and Gina handed him a sterile towel to dry his wet hands. When he was gowned and gloved, he stood in front of the table, staring at the set up.

Ignoring Gina, he spoke to the patient, "We're going to start now. You just close your eyes and before you know it, we'll be all through."

The patient mumbled something. Tallent said to Gwen, "Good job."

Chapter 27

"I couldn't believe it, "Gina said to Harry. "Mort Tallent never said a word about Lolly or me wandering through his office. Not one word."

"How did he treat you?" Harry took a huge bite of his taco; sauce dripped from the bottom, covering a good portion of his plate with thick, red salsa.

"Standoffish, condescending. Definitely looking for any little glitch he could pin on me. You know, read me the riot act about some nonexistent thing that almost killed the patient."

"You're good." Harry wiped off the sauce, which had now dribbled onto his wrist. He took her hand. "And, you're one lucky woman."

"I guess the question is, why didn't he speak up? I know there's something screwy going on with Tallent, bookkeeper or no bookkeeper. We need to get to the bottom of it."

"Where did that *we* come from?" Harry looked at his watch. She knew it was getting close to the end of their lunch break. He finished up the remains of his taco. "I told you I didn't want any part of this whole business right from the beginning."

"Have you found a hacker for us yet?"

"Man, did you even hear one thing I said? Besides, we just talked about it. Give me a chance. One of us has to think about consequences. That's one big, dangerous step hacking into someone's computer files. I'm not exactly into the federal prison thing. They toss you in there and throw away the key, even for white-collar crimes." He chuckled. "Besides, it would mess up our wedding plans."

"Oh, hell, people hack into stuff all the time." Gina used her fork to push salad from one part of the plate to another."

"Not like you to skip lunch." Harry pointed to her dish full of food.

"I'm still kind of keyed up."

Harry moved his chair closer to her, nuzzled her neck, kissed her cheek. "I'll bet you were great in that OR. Believe me, if you weren't, you would have heard."

"Get a room," her brother Vinnie said, pulling up a chair and setting his tray on the table. "Harry, you have to learn to keep your hands to yourself."

Harry gave Vinnie a wide smile. "Not on your life."

"I swear, Vin, don't you ever eat anything other than hamburgers and French fries?" Gina reached across the table and stole one of the fries and dipped it into the spread of catsup that covered a quarter of the plate.

"Hey, when I love something, I never give up on it." Vinnie pointed a fry at her. "Otherwise, I'd have gotten rid of you long ago."

"Ha, ha." She snatched the fry from his finger tips and stuck it in her mouth. "Where's Helen?"

"Taking a later lunch. Too busy to hang out with her fiancée."

Gina looked up and caught a man with piercing eyes staring at her. Actually, she'd noticed him on and off throughout lunch, but hadn't thought anything about it. He was in no hurry to turn away when he saw her looking back at him.

Harry stood. "Short, but sweet. I have a lot of really sick ones in ICU. Better get going." He leaned over and kissed Gina goodbye. "See you later, beautiful."

She watched Harry walk away, agilely slipping between the crowded tables. Just watching him made her chest swell with happiness.

How did I ever get so lucky to find this Lucke guy?

Then her eyes found the man again. He was still watching her.

* * *

Mort Tallent was relieved at the end of the cardio cath procedure. When he'd placed the stent in the artery, he couldn't stop his hand from shaking. It was fortunate everything turned out okay.

All I need is to poke an arterial vessel and shoot off a clot to the brain or the lungs.

Having Gina scrub in with him had made him nervous and unsure. It was as though she were scrutinizing his every move—which he'd expect every good scrub nurse to do. But this was different.

He'd started out wanting to put her on the defensive from the moment he knew she would be assisting him. But in the end, he was the one who felt insecure about how to proceed with questioning her about the break-in with Lolly.

Back in his office he'd refused to go out for lunch. Instead, he heated a can of tomato soup in their kitchen, took it to his office, and closed the door. Both Bob and Jon had indicated earlier that they wanted to talk to him about something. At the moment, he didn't want to talk to anyone ... about anything.

He sat behind his desk and stared at the bowl of hot soup—soon the tiny plumes of steam slowed and disappeared. He made himself take a spoonful.

Now, it was almost room temperature.

He leaned back into his chair, tried to take deep breaths to relax, but suddenly he was sobbing; his chest heaved and he gasped for air. Without thinking, he opened the bottom desk drawer and pulled out a picture of Annie.

He stared at her beautiful face. She'd had a smile that melted his heart.

He hadn't looked at this picture for a long time and thought he should get rid of it. He'd thought that before, but every time he started to toss it, he stopped and tucked it back in the desk drawer.

Why did she have to fall out of love with me when I loved her so much?

And why did he always ask himself the same question when he already knew the answer?

When money became more important than her, or anything else, he'd lost her. And he knew what he was doing, but he couldn't stop himself. It was as though the money would justify his giving up the things he'd lived for before he became a physician.

Fucking fool!

His whole relationship with a killer started with Annie. He'd allowed Vlad to push him over the edge, arrange for her killing—and it hadn't stopped there. He'd also arranged for his bookkeeper Maria, and in the end, her mother, to die. All at the hands of Vlad.

It was Maria's own fault. Yes, she'd brought it on herself. All she had to do was her job. It wasn't up to her to question his practice, to question why he padded and created Medicare costs that didn't exist. That he'd gone ahead charging for procedures that were cancelled.

Did she have a right to question the extent of his charges? They were his, not hers.

No! All she needed to do was keep the accounts straight. That was her job and if she'd done that, and only that, there would have been no need for Vlad to step in.

He couldn't even begin to think about what that maniac did to Lolly to get her to leave town. Her resume said she'd come from the Bronx—probably taken off and gone back East.

Now, there was Gina Mazzio. Another Bronx bitch. Vlad would probably want to take care of her, too, even though Tallent had said to let it go.

But how do you stop a stone-cold killer once he's been let out of the cage?

Chapter 28

Kat Parker sat in the Golden Eye Tech employee cafeteria, across from Cal Cortez. The timing had been difficult, but they'd finally managed to match up their lunch hours. Without thinking about it, they'd both ended up with a Cobb salad, which they were discreetly feeding to each other and laughing. The place was very crowded so they kept a business-like distance, too far to hold hands under the table, which is what Kat really wanted to do.

Thoughts of her future medical procedure plagued her and she knew she should tell Cal about the upcoming surgery. They'd talked about everything else and it was continually popping into her head—she wanted to tell him, but she was sure it would scare him away.

Who wants to get into a new relationship with someone who's sick?

If they'd known each other longer, had some kind of history together, well, maybe it would have been an easier choice. But they'd just found each other. It seemed like forever since she'd felt so close to another person. She couldn't bear the thought of him shutting her out for *any* reason.

Is this really me? Cautious, self-conscious me? Allowing myself to fall for someone in the blink of an eye?

When they'd made love, she'd forgotten she was no longer young, that she was fat. He'd made her feel so beautiful, and important.

She couldn't help but notice how handsome he was in his soft brown sport shirt—it matched his coco-colored eyes. When she looked at his wavy brown hair, she blushed, flashing on the moment she'd clutched a massive tuft of it, lost in an orgasm. Was he remembering that moment, too, because his face had tinged pink and he smiled at her with dreamy eyes?

"Would you like to have dinner at my house tonight?" she asked, freeing a foot from her shoe, rubbing it across his calf.

"I would love that." He put his fork down and looked at her with his soft eyes. "I can't begin to tell you how much our time together means to me. All I want to do is reach across the table and touch you all over."

Kat thought her heart would burst. "Me, too."

"I'm not exactly sure what's happening, but truthfully, I'd given up finding anyone like you."

He was so calm, so serene, so earnest, she couldn't help but believe him. "Anyone?"

"Kat, I've been divorced for ten years. I've dated a lot, an awful lot—meeting people on-line, through friends. You name it, I've done it." He reached for her hand across the table. "But never once has there been the kind of instant spark that you and I have."

"And I'd kind of given up, too, of ever falling in love again." She couldn't help it, she squeezed his hand tightly.

Her iPhone, sitting on the end of the table, buzzed. She glanced at the cell's window, saw it was from Dr. Tallent's office.

It must be for the pre-op appointments.

She let the call go to her message box. The last thing she wanted to do was discuss her future appointments in front of Cal.

* * *

Kat was back in her office staring at the scatter of notes on her desk reminding her of all the projects she had to work on. Right now, she didn't feel like tackling any of it. She was still under the spell of her lunch time with Cal.

She stared at her cell. She'd listened to the lunchtime message, knew she had to call the doctor's office and make her appointments. If she was going to start a new relationship, she wanted to know where she stood with her health.

Might as well get this over with.

"Drs. Tallent, Cantor, and Brichett's office. May I help you?"

"Yes, hi. This is Kat Parker, returning you call."

"Good afternoon, Ms. Parker. I was calling to set up your pre-op appointments. Can you possibly come in tomorrow at two for your physical and blood work?"

She wanted to scream, no!

"How long will all that take?"

"About an hour."

"If I must, I must."

The receptionist responded with an expected laugh. "I'm afraid so."

"Yes, I can work that out. I'll see you tomorrow at two."

* * *

Mulzini was staring at the television, had been for the last half hour. He couldn't tell you what movie he'd been watching—couldn't even remember who the characters were, or what was what in the dumb plot. That's the way it had been since he saw the doctor. He had trouble concentrating on anything for more than a few minutes.

He'd always been okay with the idea of dying. After all, he was a cop—his number could come up at any moment.

But that was on the job. Now he had to stare down his mortality in a different light—he'd chosen to look death in the face, head-on, and it was pock-marked and charred with time.

Why the hell did I insist on the procedure? Why not limp along? Keep taking tests?

Probably the easiest question to answer he'd ever asked himself.

That's not me, you idiot!.

Marcia had stayed out of his way as much as possible. Right now, she was in her studio painting. A couple of hours ago, he'd helped her carry in a large batch of pre-stretched canvasses she'd found on sale. He'd complained all the way into the apartment. Not only that, she'd run out of a lot of her favorite colors and the tube-filled bags of pigment seemed endless.

Wasn't he supposed to worry about lugging things? Guess not. That doc didn't seem to think so.

He'd made a dumb comment to Marcia, "What are you painting? The Sistine Chapel?"

Bad move.

She'd looked at him with stony eyes that made him cringe.

After everything was set up in her studio and he'd turned and walked away, there was no *thank you* to follow him out the door.

Women! I'll never understand them.

Chapter 29

Robert Cantor and Jon Brichett were waiting for Tallent when he finished hospital rounds and returned to his office. They'd been trying to talk to him for days, and until now he'd successfully dodged being cornered. He looked at the two men and knew he was in for a rough ride.

"Sorry to barge in like this," Cantor said, standing next to his desk. "But it's way past time we had that talk we've been asking for."

"And good afternoon to you, too," Tallent said.

"Hey, now don't get all up tight, Mort," Brichett said. "We haven't gotten together to talk about the practice for ages."

"Yeah, well, take me out to dinner, wine and dine me, and I'll call that a great meeting." Tallent hung his jacket in the small office closet and shrugged on his white coat for his patient visits. "But this feels more like a gang bang."

"Just like you to always go for the gonads," Cantor said. "But if it's anything, it's more like an intervention ... so I'll just lay it on the line and we'll get into it."

Tallent walked behind his desk and sat down. "What do you want?"

"Look, we're here as colleagues," Brichett said, smiling. "It's just that—well, let's face it, since Annie died, you haven't been yourself."

"What you mean is, since Annie took off with another man and divorced me. Isn't that what you really want to say?"

Brichett looked away.

"Okay, I'm going to dump the whole thing in your lap," Cantor said. "You're a real ass and I'm not going to pussyfoot around with you."

"No one ever accused you of zipping it up." Tallent moved some papers around on his desk, trying to calm himself.

127

"What the hell is going on?" Cantor leaned over the desk until he was practically in Tallent's face. "You're overbooking, overusing the Cath Lab."

"Are you forgetting that the equipment and facility privileges are here for all three of us?" Trying to stall, Tallent looked at Jon Brichett, who sat down in one of the chairs—it was obvious he wasn't about to dive into this.

"That's right. It does belong to the three of us, but I have to wait to get on the schedule. It takes so long I have to use Ridgewood when I shouldn't have to."

"We've never fought over this before," Tallent said. "Why now?"

"Well, hell's bells, you're certainly not losing any money, but my receivables are beginning to look like shit." Cantor paused for a moment. "Look, Mort, besides all that, you're not yourself. You're walking around with your head up your ass."

Tallent jumped to his feet. "Get out of here!"

Brichett rushed over to Cantor. "Bob, cut that out. You don't have to be rude."

"Maybe I do, Jon. Seems it's the only way I can get this man's attention." Cantor turned back to Tallent. "Listen, I'm sorry about the outburst, but we're worried about you. You don't seem to be yourself."

Tallent sat back down in his chair, covered his face with his hands. He swallowed hard, tried to regain his composure. Finally, he looked up at Cantor.

"Look, I know I'm not the easiest person in the world to get along with. I wish I could be more like the two of you. But I can't. That's just not my nature."

"Hell, Mort, you don't have to be like us," Brichett said. "But you do need to calm down. You need a break from the practice. It would do you a world of good. When was the last time you took a vacation?"

Tallent turned away from his partners, looked out the window at the city below. When had he'd done something more soothing than just looking out the window—for even a whole day or more? It was either work or living inside his head.

"I don't know." Tallent turned back to the two of them. "You're right. I need to get away."

Cantor visibly relaxed, his shoulders eased down.

Tallent looked at the two men—Cantor, calmer, but still hot under the collar; Brichett, concerned. "Give me some time to think about it." He paused. "Meanwhile, I'll finish up the active cases I have for the next two weeks and go from there."

Both men nodded at him and left his office.

* * *

The minute Gina and Harry walked into the apartment, she grabbed up her land line and punched in Lolly's number. It'd been hard to concentrate at her job. Two or three times every day she'd tried to reach Lolly, without success. All her calls had gone to message mode.

"It's ringing," she said to Harry. "I hope she's there this time, I need to speak to her—I'm really worried."

After four rings, the phone was finally picked up, but no one spoke. Gina heard ragged breathing on the other end.

"Hello. Hello!" Gina said. "Lolly, are you there?" She had pressed the speaker phone button so Harry could listen in. Gina's question echoed across the living room. Harry sat down on the sofa next to her.

"Hello, Gina."

It was Lolly—her voice flat and lifeless.

"What happened to you? You disappeared—left your job, your apartment, without a word. I've been trying to call you forever."

The line was silent for a long time. At first Gina thought Lolly had hung up, but she could still hear her breathing.

Goosebumps rode up Gina's arms.

"Do you remember how you were after Dominick beat you?" Lolly said, her voice low and lifeless. "After you lost so much blood, we all thought you were going to die." Lolly's heavy breathing was louder than her voice. "You were so hurt you didn't care whether you lived or died."

Chills rode up and down Gina's body. It was a moment before she could answer. "Yes, of course I do." Tears welled in her eyes, rolled down her cheeks. "I'll never forget any of it."

Harry's stricken face stared back at her. He wrapped his arms around her, held on tight.

"Well, that's the way I was when I left San Francisco."

"Who hurt you?" Gina said, crying. All she could do was picture herself back in a Bronx hospital after her ex had beaten her to within an inch of her life. There wasn't a part of her body that hadn't been in pain.

"I don't know who he was."

"When? How?" Gina couldn't stop herself. She had to know.

"He snatched me at my car in the underground garage after work," she said in the voice of someone watching a far away reel of information scrolling through her brain.

"He tied me up. My God, he terrorized me, beat me. Raped me." Lolly began to sob. The words came in short burst. "He cut me...cut up my whole body."

Gina and Harry were both crying with her.

"Oh, Lolly. Is somebody taking care of you?"

"I don't want to see anyone."

"I can fly back, be there with you." Gina was gulping, could hardly get the words out.

"I'll come, too, Lolly." Harry said. "We can both help."

"No! No one can help me. I don't want to be with anyone right now. She started crying again. "I just want to be in a dark room where it's peaceful and quiet so I can stop thinking about dying."

Gina looked at Harry. He shook his head.

"Listen, both of you. This has to do with breaking into Tallent's office." Her voice became desperate. "Stay away from that man or you'll become a target, too."

"Lolly! Lolly!"

But Lolly was gone.

* * *

Vlad strutted around, naked. He liked feeling free, he liked the air rushing over his body as he wandered around his apartment.

He ambled into his bedroom. It was clean, cleared of any unnecessary furniture. He looked at the small table behind the headboard where he kept all the different blades lined up according to size. All of them spotless, cleaned to a shine ... except for one.

He'd kept the knife that he'd used on Tallent's nurse, as is. It was still bloody. The blood had turned black and was splattered across the handle. It had been there too long. Cleaning it would now require soaking. But that's the way he liked it—that's the way he held onto the memory.

It was a ritual he couldn't seem to break. But when a blade was black, uneasiness again began to curl in his groin. Nothing eased it—nothing except sex and the slicing of skin. Female skin.

He re-straightened everything, even though it had already been neat. He carried the used, bloody blade to the bathroom sink. He ran water over it, put it down very carefully, and squirted detergent on it, from the butt of the handle to the tip of the blade.

He thought of the two women on the security tapes from Tallent's office.

The blonde with the long hair and blue eyes was gone. He'd seen her run away. Too bad the good doctor hadn't wanted her killed.

It had been difficult not to plunge the knife down deeper into the layers of skin that were like butter. Hard not to kill her.

But the other one, the dark-haired one he'd tracked to Ridgewood Hospital, she was different, she didn't work for Tallent.

Vlad pictured her flawless, slender body tied up and ready.

Chapter 30

Harry let Gina out in front of their apartment building and drove off to see his brother. She found it weird to think that Paul Lucke was involved with hackers, a group of people she held in fairly low esteem. They made her think of sabotage, cyber viruses, and generally doing very destructive things.

Yet, here she was looking for a hacker to help save people's lives.

Amazing how prejudices diminish when you need something for yourself.

She looked up and down the street, for no particular reason, while fishing around in her huge purse for her apartment key. She stopped when she saw a tall man across the street, leaning against a tree. He was staring at her. Her heart skipped a beat when she realized it was the same man she'd seen in the Ridgewood cafeteria.

When he saw her looking at him, he quickly turned away. Also, there was something off about his body language. He wasn't only waiting, he wasn't only looking. He was hunting.

Her eye immediately sent out a warning twitch and her New York instincts went into full alarm. Her fingers curled around the house key and she slipped through the entry in minimum time. She hurried up the steps to their apartment. After double-locking the door, she ran to the window to take another look at the man.

He was gone.

* * *

Vlad had carefully surveyed the small car and driver that dropped off Gina Mazzio. The two of them had kissed before he drove off. He'd seen that same man with her at the hospital cafeteria. That could complicate things. But she was definitely the other woman who'd appeared with Lolly Stentz on the security tape from Tallent's office.

After he snatched Lolly Stentz in the underground garage, he had been certain that cutting and fucking her would be sufficient to make her give up the name of her partner. But the bitch wouldn't do it, no matter how much he slashed her. He'd wanted to cut up her face, but he knew that would send her running to the police.

Vlad didn't like failure. He'd wanted to kill that Lolly woman, but Tallent had said, no, and the doctor paid him a lot of money in the past—he might be good for more cash in the future. So, Vlad let her go. It gave him some satisfaction that she'd never be very attractive in the nude again and that he was the last man to see how beautiful she was.

If there was one thing he d learned growing up on the streets, there was a solution to every problem—you only had to be willing to wait to find it. Vlad was forced to move on when the nurse wouldn't talk. The next step was to bully his way into Tallent's apartment, where the good doctor caved and gave him Gina Mazzio's name; told him everything he wanted to know about her.

Once he found her in Ridgewood Hospital, it didn't take much to wait and follow her home from work.

Too bad there was a man involved. They always got in the way.

* * *

Mort Tallent stood at the water's edge, taking in deep breaths, trying to absorb the raw power of the ocean. That smell of the sea always soothed him. Standing here, his toes digging into the wet sand, made him think of his competitive surfing days.

With the sun beating down on his back, he would paddle out looking for the huge waves. Once riding the surge, he would surrender to the water that held and caressed him. It was strange, but primal, moving to a rhythm that assured he was part of everything that ever was or ever would be—he became a human at one with the earth, at one with the vast universe.

He thought of those moments often. Old memories. Good memories.

Now, his feet were cold and the water washing up to his ankles was icy. The days had turned shorter and after working hours, it was dark, with only a sliver of the moon allowing him to see a small segment of a world he couldn't stop remembering.

His big wave surfer's dream, Mavericks, would be happening soon. Its crazy surf breaks could pick you up and bash your body against the rocks. But he had never worried much about death when he was out there. All he wanted to do was ride a monster—wipeout or not, crushed by the ocean depths or not.

Hell, everyone dies. If it happened then, at least it would be of my own choice.

Tallent still rode the board every now and then while on vacations. The last time was with Annie when they both cried over past days when they surfed and surfed and made love in the sand under the moonlight.

Annie, Annie. I think of you more and more.

She was dead because of him and that continued to eat away at his soul. It was becoming harder to concentrate on anything. Some times in the middle of surgery, he would find himself day-dreaming about the past and how he'd lost the love of his life.

He slowly walked back to the sea wall and tried to wipe away the loose sand clinging to his feet.

Maybe it was time to slam the door on his medical career. He had enough money—that wasn't his problem at all.

The problem was his twisted soul.

* * *

Kat Parker was having trouble falling asleep. She was lying next to Cal, semi-awake. Their evening had been idyllic. After dinner, they'd sat around laughing at each other's jokes, then discussing the way they felt about life, from politics to their careers. In the end, they'd made love and he fell asleep with her curled up in his arms.

The two of them had happened so quickly—an unexpected whirlwind that landed her with a man she could emotionally connect with without reservation. And he accepted her the way she was.

She quietly sidled from the bed and wandered into the living room. Looking out the window, she worried how she was going to tell Cal about her Cardio Cath in two days.

There was no way out. She had to tell him. It would be impossible to cover up something like that. Besides, it wasn't fair not to tell him. He deserved the truth.

She jumped when he came up behind her and wrapped his arms around her waist.

"Hey, what are you doing up?" He squeezed her tighter. "I woke up and you were gone."

She turned in his arms. "I have to tell you something, Cal. Something that I probably should have told you right from the beginning." Her voice was tentative as each word stuck in her throat.

"What is it?"

Pain was building up in her neck and back—her heart was racing. "I need to have a serious medical procedure done in a couple of days."

Even in the dim light she could see the frown on his face. "What kind of procedure?"

The look on his face left her devastated. "I wanted to tell you before, but I couldn't."

"But why? What's wrong?"

She couldn't speak. The words wouldn't come. Fear was shutting her down.

He took her arm, led her to the sofa. "Tell me, Kat. Please."

She started crying, then she was sobbing, her chest heaving with pain and despair. He pulled her close, murmured, "It's all right. I'm here."

"I've been having neck and back pain for quite a while." She swiped away at the tears. "They've been following me with tests, trying to get me to lose weight, change my life style. I've really tried. But I finally gave up. I need to know if there's something wrong with my heart once and for all."

"And your doctor advised surgery?"

"My internist wanted me to work on my weight and eating habits, but I got disgusted and asked for a referral to a cardiologist."

"You know you could have told me about the procedure."

"We'd just found each other, Cal. I didn't want to lose you."

He squeezed her tighter, and then even tighter. "That's going to be a lot harder than you think. I'm not letting you go."

"You mean it?"

He leaned over and kissed her, and then kissed her again and again until she was breathless.

Chapter 31

Harry was tired—it had been a long, busy day. The stairs to his brother Paul's second floor apartment seemed to go on forever.

He missed Paul now that his brother lived in Noe Valley instead of the Sunset District where he and Gina lived.

He knocked and waited. It took a minute or two before Paul opened the door.

"Hey, thought I gave you a key. Since when did you become too timid to barge into my place at any hour?"

"Didn't want to scare the hell out of you."

"What's up, little brother?" Paul reached out and they gave each other a big bear hug.

Harry edged inside and wasn't a bit surprised by the abominable condition of the flat. Clothes were strewn everywhere and when he walked into the kitchen, the sink was overflowing with dirty dishes. A small table held a pile of empty cardboard pizza boxes.

"Paulo, what am I gonna do with you? This place is a mess. You're supposed to be a good example to me. Every older brother is supposed to be that."

"Obviously, not me." Paul offered Harry a seat on a sofa filled with books of every description.

"No way, man. You and I are cleaning up this mess before I take you out to dinner. You put those books in the case over there. Hell, this is your joint. I shouldn't have to tell you where to put things. Just do it!"

Paul started collecting the books, shoving them into the living room's wall-to-wall bookcases.

"While you're doing that, I'll start in the kitchen." Pretty soon Harry was elbow deep into suds and dishes. "How's work at the docks?"

Paul shrugged. "It's okay. It's a living." He started laughing. "It's a good thing I bought a bottle of detergent the other day or you'd really be screaming your head off." He went for the vacuum, started it.

They worked in silence, except for the roar of the appliances and the clattering of dishes. Since Paul's divorce, Harry's visits always began with the same ritual—the two of them cleaning up Paul's mess.

"Gina kick you out?" Paul put the vacuum away, gathered up another bunch of magazines from a corner of the sofa and piled them neatly in a chair he'd taken from the kitchen. "I usually don't see you around dinner time."

"Nope. In fact, I've been meaning to tell you—we're getting married in April,"

"No shit! You finally got her to agree to tie the knot?"

"You know about Dominick meeting the grim reaper, right?"

"Yeah," Paul said. "It couldn't have happened to a nicer guy. I can't imagine anyone hurting that woman of yours. Dominick dead. Wow! What a fucking loser."

"Eloquently stated ... and very true." Harry started drying the dishes and stacking them in the cupboards. "It was like the weight of the world dropped from her shoulders after that. Things have really been great since."

"She's a fine woman. Actually, a saint to put up with you." Paul went into the kitchen, started to help clean off the counters. "Have you told Mom and Dad yet?"

"No," Harry said. "I thought I'd wait so there wouldn't be too many snide shots of Mom calling her 'the little Catholic girl,' and then listening to Dad make fun of my being a nurse."

"They don't mean any harm. They're just old fashioned."

"No way, Paulo. It's mean, and so are the prejudices that fuel it."

"Were they nice to her when they met her?" Paul asked.

"Actually, I've soft-shoed my way out of doing that. " Harry scoured the sink, avoiding Paul's eyes. "Do I have to do the bathroom or have you been taking care of it?"

"Yeah, yeah. Everything's cool. I can only take so much of your nagging. You're worse than my ex was."

Harry took the dish towel and flung it onto the kitchen table. "Let's get out of here."

They went to a small, local restaurant that Paul had suggested. It served mostly American-style comfort food. Harry was eating a turkey burger with salad on the side. Paul had a twelve ounce medium-rare steak that had taken up most of the plate when it was served; a small side dish held a baked potato, loaded with sour cream and bacon bits.

"So you haven't introduced Gina to Mom and Dad?"

"Look, she has enough of a rift with her own parents, does she need to take on ours?" Harry dug his fork into the salad and took a mouthful.

Paul's eyes turned hard. "Yeah, I remember her folks rode her back for leaving her ex, even after he nearly killed her."

"You know, it's the Italian bit—her parents are friends with Dominick's parents from the old country."

"Yeah, parents can be a real pain in the ass. " Harry watched Paul chew his steak slowly and glance up at him every few seconds..

"All right, Harry." Paul let his fork drop to the plate. "Spit it out! You're holding back and it's not about your wedding plans. I'm here for you, man ... long as it doesn't have anything to do with putting up any money. In fact, I was thinking of calling you for a short-term loan."

"You're so full of bullshit, Paulo, don't know how you can stand living with yourself."

"Cause no one else will have me."

"And you have no idea what causes that?"

"Gee, not a clue." He snorted a laugh. "Anyway, what's the favor?"

Harry stalled by taking another bite of his burger, chewed it long past the time necessary to swallow it. "I need your help and I don't know exactly how and what to ask for."

"This has got to be a first—you being tongue-tied. "

"It's complicated," Harry said.

"Everything's complicated. Just lay it on me."

Harry thought about it, but there was no easy way to do it. "Gina's got a problem and we need to find someone who knows how to hack computers."

Paul's mouth dropped open. "You need to hack into someone's computer?"

"Exactly," Harry said.

Paul sat back in the chair and laughed. "Well, that sounds like the Gina I know. Always getting you into some kind of shit."

Harry gave his brother the barest outline of the situation. "And we need to get into the bookkeeping files of this doctor we think is cooking the books."

"Frankly, I don't give a rat's ass," Paul said.

"Come on, Paul. Think about it. The guy's not only cheating his patients, he's putting their lives at risk."

Paul leaned over the table, brought his voice just above a whisper, "You know we could end up in jail if we go down that road."

"But we're damn sure that this doc is responsible for the murders of two people, maybe even a third."

"Harry—"

"—not only that, he's probably responsible for the rape and knifing of a nurse—a friend of Gina's. We just can't let people get away with things like that."

"Whoa, little brother. This *is* serious. Shouldn't the police be called in? "

"Realistically, yes. But in this circumstance, no."

"Oh, it's like that is it?"

"Yeah, it's like that. Anyway, you know computers, Paul, and I'd bet a bundle that you know someone who can get this kind of job done. Thing is, we need proof or the police will just bury it."

Paul leaned over the table, brought his voice down to just above a whisper, "Do I need to repeat this: We could all end up in the slammer if we go down that road."

"Yeah, I know, bro. But this is important. Gina's trying to keep people from dying."

There was a long pause. Paul took a bite of his steak, chewed it slowly. "Tell you what, I do know a couple of computer nerds down at the docks. Let me ask around, see what I can find out." He cut into his steak again "It'll be up to one of them whether to jump in or not."

"We really need your help, Paulo."

"Alright, alright already. You know I'm always here for you, little brother."

"Thanks. I owe you, man."

"Not yet. But if this works out, you will. Big time." He shoved his empty plate away, burped, and said, "I'll give you a call after I check with some guys, okay?"

"Thanks, man."

Chapter 32

Gina was spooked. She went through the apartment double-checking the latch on every window. Along the way, she opened the front door to the extent of the chain, peeked out, and relocked it at least three times. She was scared and that sinking feeling in the pit of her stomach wouldn't go away.

Harry was still out with Paul. She wanted to call him, tell him about the man outside, how she'd seen him at Ridgewood staring at her in the cafeteria when Harry was rushing back to ICU. How after that she'd sort of forgotten about it ... until she got home and he was standing there right across the street from their building.

She knew if she called Harry, he would come straight home, whether he was finished talking to Paul or not. That would leave them in limbo with the plan to hack into Tallent's computer—they needed help from Paul. She didn't know anyone with those offbeat skills, didn't even know where to begin looking.

She slipped out of her clothes, carried her pajamas and slippers to the bathroom, and turned on the water to take a hot, hot shower. Tuva the cat trailed after her with a constant meow for her dinner.

After speaking to Lolly, Gina finally realized just how much things had once again gotten out of hand. She was scared, knew *she* wasn't safe. The shower scene from *Psycho* flashed in her mind. She locked the bathroom door before stepping into the shower. No one was going to surprise her in the shower stall with a knife.

Stop it, you idiot!

She was probably as safe in her locked apartment as anyone could be. But she still couldn't stop worrying.

The bathroom was steaming and the mirror was fogged over. Gina looked down at Tuva. "Why aren't you a big German Sheppard?"

Gina could swear the cat crossed its eyes at her.

"Comedian!"

She stayed under the water, allowing it to beat down on her back for a long time. After she toweled off, she slipped into the warm pair of pajamas and her slippers, padded out to the kitchen—Tuva on her heels again, still meowing.

"All right! I'm getting your dinner."

She'd just finished feeding the cat when the phone rang. She hurried into the living room and picked up. "Hello."

Someone was breathing heavily at the other end.

"Hello!"

The screen said unidentified caller.

"I don't like these kinds of games." She slammed down the phone.

Gina stood there, chilled all over, knowing it was going to ring again.

But it didn't.

Thoughts of Lolly and what had happened to her kept rioting in her head. Lolly! All of it had to be related to their night excursion into Mort Tallent's office.

And that man she'd seen earlier was probably the one who hurt Lolly and sent her flying back home to the Bronx.

* * *

It was dark by the time Vlad came back again to scope out the nurse's apartment building. The lights were on in every window he could see. He watched residents take their keys and go inside. Everyone carefully waited for the door to click shut behind them.

He could see security cameras over the entrance, positioned to cover every angle. And it was obvious that all the trees were kept pruned so there were no limbs near the windows.

Too bad! That would have been an easy way in.

He walked up to the entrance as though he belonged there and tried the door. Locked, as he'd assumed it would be. He was focusing on the entryway behind the large glass panel in the solid wood door when he felt a presence near him. He twisted his head around and looked up at a huge bear of a man.

"Can I help you?" the man said gruffly.

"Oh, I was going to visit with a cousin of mine who's supposed to live here."

"What's the name?"

Vlad did something he rarely did: he backed away from the scowling man. He quickly looked up at the stone-carved number above the entryway.

"Now that's a bummer. I got the wrong building."

"What number were you looking for?" the man demanded.

Vlad pretended he hadn't heard the question, turned quickly, and started walking away.

* * *

Vlad was irritated that he'd had to park several blocks away from Mazzio's building. And it took extreme concentration not to look back over his shoulder to see if the giant was following him.

Should never have been caught off guard like that.

Something small and hard was jammed into the small of his back.

"You feel that?" a voice said behind him.

Before Vlad could respond, he was faced by a second man, who thrust a large hand in the middle of his chest and shoved.

He was about Vlad's height, maybe a little taller, and much heavier. Vlad kept trying to get a better look at the man, but the street light kept dimming and blinking, like it was about to blow out. Then for a long moment he could see clearly—it was one of the bouncers from a place where he liked to play Pai Gow. Last time he'd lost—big time.

"What's your problem," Vlad snarled.

A hammer-like fist slammed into his nose. Vlad staggered, felt blood streaming down across his lips, saw it drop to the sidewalk in big globs.

"Give me anymore shit, and that guy with a gun in your back is going to blow you away." He waited a beat. "Do hear what I'm saying, smart mouth?"

"Yeah ... I hear." Vlad was dizzy and his legs felt weak. That had never happened to him before. "Whattaya want, you and your friend?"

"Fuck's sake! Are you stupid? We want the money you owe. We're not here looking to dance with you."

Hands held high, Vlad was about to risk popping the guy in front of him in the mouth and take his chances with the one jamming the gun into his back, but his body was limp and too slow to respond.

He looked around. The street was deserted. Not one soul out for a walk.

"Okay. Okay! Give me a moment to get my wallet out."

"Not a chance, buster. We'll take care of that for you."

From behind, one hip was patted, then the other. "Nothing here," said the gunman. The man in front reached into Vlad's inside jacket pocket and pulled out his tri-fold wallet, gave him a steely-eyed glare, and opened up the folded leather. "Well, looks like we got something here." He flipped through the bills and said, "Gotta be five grand in the wallet."

"That's a start," said the gunman. "Where's the other twenty, loser?"

"Listen..."

Vlad never finished. A huge fist, wrapped in brass knuckles, slammed into his face. He tried to pull back but the bouncer hit him again. He dropped to one knee, and then went all the way down. As he rolled over, he glimpsed another one of the Pai Gow brutes standing over him, pointing a semi-automatic.

"Bang, bang," the man said and laughed. He kicked Vlad in the ribs, stooped down and went through his pockets. He found Vlad's keys to his apartment and car, kicked him once more, and was gone.

* * *

Tuva finished her tin of boutique cat food while Gina stared at the table and her cooling bowl of homemade soup. She loved soup, especially her own Italian–style mix of vegetables and noodles. This batch had been sitting in the fridge for a couple of days—all the seasoning had now inundated everything, making it lip-licking wonderful.

She'd planned on finishing off the soup with Harry tonight, but here she sat, toying with it, letting her spoon dip through the mixture without raising it to her mouth.

What do I do now?

Everything that happened to Lolly kept running through her head.

At the very center was Tallent. His misuse of medical power that hurt patients while at the same time lined his pockets with their money. Of course, it was all supposition. Still, she just knew it was true.

Had he been responsible for the murders of his bookkeeper, Maria Benz, and her mother?

Had he been the one who caused his ex wife's death? That was the scuttlebutt at Ridgewood.

Was he actually a murderer? Or was it the man who assaulted Lolly and was now following her?

Anywhere she started, it all ended with Morton Tallent, MD.

Bette Golden Lamb & J. J. Lamb

Chapter 33

"Hi, Marcia. This is Gina Mazzio."

Marcia started laughing. "You don't have to tell me who it is. Two words out of your mouth and that Bronx accent burns up my land line."

"Nah, you're just teasing ... like Mulzini does ... just to get a rise out of me."

"That, too. You want to speak to him?"

"How's he doing?"

The line went dead for a long moment. "The truth? He's depressed as hell. Thinks his life is over. In general, miserable and not too great to be around ... all the time."

"Poor Mulzini."

"Heck. Poor me! I've never seen him like this." Marcia lowered her voice. "He usually gets a big kick out of watching me paint—teasing me until I have to throw him out, but he hasn't come into my studio once since he saw the doctor."

"Mulzini not teasing *is* strange."

"I'm really worried about him."

"Maybe I shouldn't bother him."

"Gina, you could be just what he needs."

* * *

"Yeah, Bronx, what do *you* want?"

"Happy to hear your voice, too." Marcia was right: Mulzini wasn't himself. "Called to see how you're doing."

"Mazzio, this is Mulzini. Remember? So stop the song and dance. I know you, and you never call without a reason, good or bad." Mulzini finally gave a quiet chuckle. "Who's trying to kill you now?"

"Hey, that's not fair."

"The hell it's not."

"Well, it seems ..."

"Stop beating around the bush and tell me about it." Mulzini's voice had picked up volume and she could tell he was interested.

She was careful, told him about her suspicions, without naming Mort Tallent.

"Mazzio, you're always good for a belly laugh."

"What do you mean?

"I'm serious," he said. "How do you do it?"

"Okay, Mulzini, I don't like where you're going with this. But, I'll ask anyway: do what?"

"Always find the creeps in this world."

He was laughing so hard, she wanted to hang up on him.

"Man, if they're out there—you'll find 'em."

"Yeah, well if the cops would find them first and get rid of them, I wouldn't have this kind of trouble always falling into *my* lap." Gina had started out joking, but now she was close to tears.

"Hey, it's all right. Like Marcia says, sometimes I go overboard. I'm sorry, kid. But a doctor?"

"They may not be the usual suspects, but it could only be him."

"Who's the doc?"

Gina hesitated, finally said, "No names. Just looking for a fresh take on the situation. You know, a hypothetical."

"Lay it on me."

"Well, just suppose you're one of those greedy people who puts money ahead of everything else."

Mulzini laughed. "Lots of those around."

"Are you going to let me tell this or not?"

"My lips are zipped."

"This particular doctor has been pushing procedures on patient to line his pockets—"

"—so what else is new?" he said. "He just wants to make the big bucks like everyone else."

"Mulzini, you're not thinking it through. Pushing surgeries on patients who don't really need them can kill them. There are all kinds of risks with any procedure."

"I get what you're saying, kid, but the worst thing in this scenario is an occasional death and unethical behavior. It sure doesn't float my boat."

"What if there was murder involved?" Gina lowered her voice. "What if this person killed someone to cover it up."

"You're talking about Dr. Mort Tallent's bookkeeper and her mother, aren't you?"

Gina didn't know what to say. "Well, I—"

"—you're going to have to get up a lot earlier to slip something past me." He barked out a terrible grunt. "Think I'm in a vacuum just because I'm not in the office?"

"I don't understand. Why would you go to him to be treated?"

"Let's get one thing straight, Mazzio: I like the guy. He treated me like a thinking person, not like some geek he was going to cut up. I'm a good judge of character and he seemed on the up and up, not that I'm ever going to like anyone passing tubes through me."

"Catheters," Gina said.

"Catheters, schmatheters. It's all the same."

"What if you're wrong, Mulzini? Wouldn't it be better to change doctors? If you won't do it for yourself or Marcia or Dirk, do for me. Do it so I can sleep nights."

"Do you know what it took for me to go to a doctor in the first place? I mean for something other than to pull a slug from my tender body? I'm not changing anything. I want this over and done with so I can get on with my life."

"Mulzini—"

"—if he *is* guilty, like you seem to think he is, you better believe I'm going to be treated with kid gloves—he wouldn't want *anything* to happen to a cop."

"I can't even begin to tell you how illogical that kind of thinking is. Besides, there's more to it—"

"—Mazzio!" His voice had turned loud and mean. "I don't want to hear anymore about this scenario you've cooked up. I always enjoy hearing from you, but not this time."

"Mulzini—"

"—goodnight, Mazzio!"

* * *

Vlad woke up, nose flat against the sidewalk, stuffed behind plastic trash cans. Every part of his body ached when he tried to sit up. He took in the stink of garbage with every breath, reminding him of the years he lived on the streets.

He tried to get up from the ground, but his legs refused to support his body; it took several minutes hanging onto a refuse bin before he could take a step.

When he started to move, pain radiated across his chest and his head was shooting flames until he thought he would go blind. He tried to slow his panicked breathing as he reached into his pocket and found his cash-empty wallet. His ID was still inside, although his only credit card was gone.

They'd dumped him behind the trash, down the street, from Lolly's friend, Gina Mazzio.

His phone was on the sidewalk and it took every bit of strength to reach down and snatch it up. The window was badly scratched but it looked usable.

Bastards probably left it for me to get my ass out of here without bringing the police in.

Holding onto the bin, he looked at the few numbers he had embedded into his contacts. The number for the health club receptionist, Rosia, popped up. One day he'd allowed her to punch it into his contacts, mainly to get her off his back. He tapped onto her number.

"Yeeesss?" Rosia answered.

"Hello." Vlad's throat was clogged, he could barely speak. "Rosia, I need your help."

"Vlad?"

"Yes. I've been robbed and beaten. Could you come and get me?"

Her voice was suspicious. "You sound very strange. Where are you?"

"I'm in the Sunset. I can't drive. I need your help."

"Didn't I tell you the day would come when you would want me?"

"Will you come? Please?"

"Darling, anything for you."

Vlad gave her the address. When he hung up, Gina Mazzio's face filled his head.

She's going to be sorry. Very sorry.

Bette Golden Lamb & J. J. Lamb

Chapter 34

Vlad was desperate when he called Rosia—he didn't think she would agree to come for him. But she not only came, she practically carried him to her car and drove him to her apartment.

He could barely breathe and every part of him hurt, but the bitch seemed to enjoy it. She sang the whole time they were in the car.

The moment he crossed the threshold of her apartment, he could smell her cheap perfume, even with a broken nose. It made him stop in his tracks and bend over with the dry heaves. He looked around the small, shabby apartment: the place was a mess with frilly clothes scattered everywhere.

Rosia was not only tough, she was rough. She dragged him into her small bathroom, studied his nose before readying strips of tape, and then without a word of warning, realigned his broken nose. It crunched into place and she taped it firmly while he screamed curses at her.

He knew he was filthy from rolling on the ground. She stripped him, shoved him into the shower, and washed him from head to toe, taking a moment to play with his limp penis. She sang throughout it all; sang so loud and off key that he thought he would pass out.

She studied his bruised and swollen face, the colors covering his broken nose. "Poor Vlad. I'm sorry to say, you will no longer be a beautiful man. Too bad."

He spent an agonizing night soaked in sweat and any movement made him want to curl up in agony. Rosia only had one bed, with a mattress so soft he kept rolling against her, making him cry out at each contact. His ribs became separate entities that reacted painfully with every breath.

When morning finally came, Vlad felt like a wasted old man, triple his thirty-two years. While Rosia fixed him breakfast, she said, "I went through your wallet. I see you have no money, darling."

"I had money. The men who beat me up stole every dollar."

"But you do have more, right?"

He nodded.

"That's what I thought, otherwise you would be back out the door. I expect to be paid for my trouble. Understand?"

He understood all right. What *she* didn't understand was that he wasn't so weak that he couldn't strangle her right in her own apartment.

* * *

The alarm went off and Gina crawled out of bed as though she was in a basin full of thick mud; her arms felt like they weighed fifty pounds each.

Harry, usually the first one up, didn't budge until she poked at his arm, again and again.

"I'll do it. I'll do it," he mumbled. 'Five minutes more. I promise." Then he was back to snoring.

In a daze, she padded into the kitchen and put together the fixings for the coffee gods and pressed the start button on the machine.

Then it hit her: This whole business about the man who was following her, that whole business with Mulzini—she'd needed to talk to Harry about it, had waited for him until after midnight, then went to bed and was asleep in an instant.

The aroma of coffee started to waft its way down the hall and into the bedroom. Gina watched Harry push himself up into a sitting position, grumping with each inch of progress.

"Oh, jeez, a night with Paulo is enough to kill me."

"Beer, beer, beer?"

"Yeah, and a few belts of tequila in between." He was inching along as he went into the bathroom.

After a few minutes, she heard his toothbrush humming away and she walked in as he was putting the sonic brush back into its charging stand.

"Paul knows someone who might do the hacking for us." He started washing his face and his words came in fits and starts. "Talk ... will—"

"—will call us?" Gina finished.

Harry reached for his shaving gear. "Yeah, that's the deal."

He was wide awake now and looked closely at Gina. "What's the matter, doll?"

"It can wait until later."

"No you don't." He took hold of her shoulders and looked into her eyes. "We said we wouldn't keep secrets from each other. What is it?"

"Remember what happened to Lolly?"

"Of course, how could I forget?"

"I think I know the man who did it."

He wrapped an arm around her and they walked back to the bedroom and sat on the edge of the bed. "Tell me."

"There was this creepy looking guy sitting in the cafeteria at Ridgewood yesterday, just staring at me." Gina gulped down the returning fear she'd been feeling. "He had no food at his table and he never took his eyes off of me."

"Babe, I stare at you all the time. You're a damn good-looking woman."

"I don't think it was that. It was kinda strange, but I really didn't get hooked into it ... then. When you dropped me off to go the Paul's, he was here, across the street, leaning against a tree, and following my every move. Scary!"

"Why didn't you call me?"

"We needed the help from Paul. That seemed more important." She sat up taller. "Besides, there was no way he could get into our apartment."

"I always thought that too," he said, "at least until last year when that stalker climbed a tree, crawled into our guestroom, and almost killed Helen."

"No one's getting in climbing a tree anymore," Gina said with a mirthless laugh. "Not unless they're Spider Man."

"I know you, babe. You were freaked out. Go pull that Bronx-toughie act on someone else." He pulled her into his arms. "Maybe you should give Mulzini a call. At least run it by him. He might have some ideas."

"I tried that, but he's not doing too well with this upcoming procedure. He needs to help himself."

"Wait a minute. Did you tell him about Tallent? That would not be too cool." Harry was obviously agitated. "In fact, it's bad enough that the doc has those tapes of you and Lolly sneaking around in his office. Bad-mouthing him to Mulzini might put him over the top."

"I didn't tell him about Tallent. He figured it out himself."

Gina watched the blood drain from Harry's face. "It's going to look bad when Mulzini goes looking for another doc for treatment."

"He's not going to do that," Gina said. "Stubborn. He's not afraid and wants to get everything over with. Right now they could cut him up in tiny pieces and he wouldn't care as long as he can put it behind him."

"I guess we really do need to get into Tallent's computer," Harry said. "It's the only way we can look at everyone's records, including Mulzini's, to see if he's really sick or having a procedure that could kill him."

Chapter 35

Alexander Yurev was growing restless.

He looked at his watch: 1:00 p.m., on the dot.

He'd been sitting in his car for three hours, watching and waiting. Still no sign of his target.

He pulled a pack of cigarettes from the glove compartment, shook his head in disgust. He'd already gone through half a pack since six this morning. His throat was dry and scratchy. A cough that was once just an occasional thing, had turned into a frequent, everyday hack. He shook his head, pulled out one cigarette, lit it with a gold lighter he kept on the seat next to him, and tossed the rest of pack back into the glove box. He inhaled and held it until he was dizzy. Only then did he release the smoke.

Was this Vlad Folo really the man he was looking for? Was he the child of Nadya and Ivan Pushkin—dead for twenty years?

He laughed to himself.

That hadn't even been their real names. Their real family name was Antonev. It didn't matter what name they were using, he'd found them anyway. What he'd failed to do twenty years ago was kill their twelve-year-old son. His boss hadn't liked that loose thread.

That's what the pig always said, 'Alex, you left a loose thread.'

He forced an even longer drag on his cigarette.

Since that day, he was smeared as if he were covered in black tar. That one mistake, that lapse meant a demotion to a low-level nothing. He would never be allowed to move up in the ranks until it was corrected.

One fucking mistake.

He'd been left behind to kill the boy—who was now a man.

* * *

That day twenty years ago was seared into Alexander Yurev's memory. A sigh escaped his lips, along with a stream of smoke.

His partner, Misha, had been a stupid man. Killing the father should have been a quick, easy kill. But Misha wanted blood. He kept beating the man.

"Where is your son, you fuckin' traitor?"

"I have no son. He died last year."

The woman wouldn't shut up. "Leave my husband alone. Please stop hurting him."

Misha wouldn't stop. "You liar. I've been in your boy's room. He has a lot of clothes and books for a dead kid." He pounded more on the tied-up man's face, then his gut. "We're gonna find him ... and kill him. He'll suffer. I promise you that he'll suffer."

"Please, please stop hurting him."

Alex knew the couple would never give up their son. He lost it then, had screamed out to Misha, "We came here to do a job. Do it!."

He was in charge, yet, Misha ignored him.

"Please! Please! Please!" The woman was driving him crazy.

Something snapped. He grabbed the woman, stripped off her clothes, cut up the bed sheets, and tied her to the frame. He tried to stop, but looking at her body made him instantly hard. She struggled to pull her arms and legs free of the knotted strips of the sheet. Her hips and pelvis twisted and turned as she fought to break loose. Her desperate efforts only stoked his lust.

He'd never raped a woman . His job was to kill. Brutish sex had nothing to do with his assignment. But he couldn't help himself. He forced himself inside of her.

Misha stopped beating the man, walked to the bed, dropped his pants, and pulled Alex away. He too, raped the woman.

Alex got into his pants, pulled out his knife, and proceeded to carry out his assignment. He slit the man's throat and immediately did the same to the woman.

When he finished, the man and woman were dead, and Misha was covered with the woman's blood.

But the boy got away—the boy who was now a man.

* * *

Alex walked up to the health club's reception desk. The same pretty tart was sitting there. Her bright red hair didn't hide the large earrings she wore. She had the same seductive smile.

"Hello, Rosia. Do you remember me? I was in a few days ago."

"I do remember you and those dark, sexy eyes." She leaned over the small desk and her full breasts lifted above the scoop-neck blouse.

"I had hoped to set up an appointment for a deep body massage with the man you suggested. Was it Vlad?"

A flash of suspicion deepened the lines in her face. He could feel her doubt, could see that she sensed something more to his request. "Let me look at his schedule."

"Thank you."

She scanned the appointment book, looked back up at him, and said, "He's very busy today, but I think I can squeeze you in, say, two weeks?"

He pulled a twenty from his pocket and tucked it under the corner of the appointment book. Her eyes lit up and a smile spread across her face. The twenty was gone in a flash.

She tapped a pencil on the desk, flipped it over to the eraser, and then flipped it back to its point and ran her index finger slowly down the center of the book. "Well, I didn't see that before—I can slip you in a week from today. Would that work for you?"

He nodded.

"What's your name?"

"Alex."

"All right, Alex. One week from today at 2 o'clock. Is there a telephone number where I can reach you? I might have an appointment available sooner?"

"That's okay. This one works into my schedule."

She gave him a come-on smile.

He let his eyes wander to her bulging breasts and returned her smile.

Chapter 36

Tallent hardly said a word as he made his rounds at Ridgewood Hospital. He moved from patient-to-patient, let them babble on about their pain, their minor complaints, how the hospital staff wasn't doing this or that, how things weren't as they should be. He nodded, smiled, said he would look into it, and moved on.

Not one word of gratitude that they're still alive. Not one word!

We save them. Them, and their dying bodies. We crack open their chests, separate bones, expose and heal their hearts. Instead of thanks, there are only complaints. They lie there, a bunch of fat cats used to getting their own way.

The nurses and their detailed notes allowed him to get a good handle on what was up with each of his patients, but he was having trouble being attentive to anyone lately.

He wandered through the CCU, watched everyone hustle, each staff person focused on the details of an assigned task. They barely paid attention to him. Even though he knew that on some level they were aware that he was there, he felt invisible, as though they could walk right through him.

He caught a glimpse of Gina Mazzio moving down a corridor toward the locker room. He turned to follow her, could almost smell her trailing scent that was cut off when she went through the door.

The lights inside the locker room were dim—an effort to rein in costs, although it probably saved very little money. He could hear her rattling a metal locker door as he walked down the aisles. They were the only ones in the deserted area.

He moved around a blind corner and saw her going through her purse. She looked up, tilted her head to one side.

"What were you and Lolly Stentz doing in my office?"

Her eyes widened, but she didn't speak.

165

"Well?"

"We were there because Lolly forgot something."

"In my office? I hardly think so." He kept looking at that soft neck of hers, imagining his fingers squeezing, cutting off her air.

"She ... she was showing me around and wanted me to see your office since she worked for you."

He could see she was uncomfortable with this whole business, but not nearly as nervous as he'd like her to be.

He took a few steps closer. "That was damn unprofessional of her to just up and quit, leave us in the lurch like that, without any notice. She left us in one helluva bad position."

"It wasn't intentional, I mean, she didn't mean to leave you hanging ... "

He moved in closer until he was no more than arm's length away. She stepped back—up against her opened locker door.

His insides were on fire. He wanted to choke the life out of her. It was eating at him, pushing him, pushing hard.

She slammed her locker door shut, turned, and hurried away.

"You'd better stay out of my way, Gina Mazzio," he yelled at her back.

* * *

Tallent raced out of the hospital, ignoring people who called out their greetings. He took the elevator down to the underground parking garage and hurried to his Mercedes AMG sedan.

Settling in, he closed his eyes and gulped deep breaths, trying to get control of his anger.

He'd wanted to choke the life out of that Gina Mazzio. She was a threat that he couldn't get away from.

What exactly did she know?

What did she and Lolly see when they sneaked into his office?

166

He leaned back and allowed his senses to take over. Every time he sat in this car it reminded him of Annie. She'd chosen it.

He stared straight ahead, seeing nothing. He could almost remember how it had smelled when it was new—leathery, rich.

And he could still catch the scent of Annie's special perfume in the interior every now and then.

* * *

He meant to drive straight to his office, but instead he drove over the Golden Gate Bridge, headed for Muir Beach in Marin County. That's where Annie liked to go. Said it was a lovely drive and it took them away from the stuffy crowds into the openness and fresh smells of the ocean.

He got off the freeway at the Mill Valley exit and went through the twisty roads that used to be so much fun to drive. There was only one other car in the Muir Beach parking lot. It was a gray day with drizzle that left tiny blobs of moisture on the surface of his highly waxed car.

He took his shoes off and walked through the icy sand up to the water's edge.

It was calm here. Off in the distance a man was throwing a stick for his dog to chase. For a moment he thought about stripping off his clothes and walking out into the sea. Tears ran down his cheeks when he remembered how Annie would dance around him, then stand on tip-toes to kiss him.

Where had it all gone wrong? He kept asking himself that question, over and over, even though the answer was one he'd always known.

He'd forgotten the man who lived in his skin. Instead, he became the man who could make money. Large amounts of money.

His mind was spinning.

It had suddenly turned warmer and the sky had become a bright blue. He could feel the sun warming his skin.

It was so good.

He kept looking at the sky as he walked into the water. He was free and the sun was hypnotic. So bright—calling to him.

"Hey, man, it's pretty cold for you to be out here."

Tallent was startled. He turned and stared at a young man dressed in a wet suit. He'd taken hold of his arm. A dog yapped at the both of them.

"Why don't we go on in now? Okay?"

He had kind eyes. Tallent saw himself, as he used to be.

"Yes, thank you. I think it's time."

Chapter 37

Gina and Harry sat at a favorite table in the cafeteria—a huge picture window that gave an open view of the hospital's atrium garden. Though most of the growth was evergreens, the bare deciduous trees and shrubs still gave the garden a snowless, wintery feeling. Rain or no rain, staring out the window always brightened her day.

When Gina first sat down, she was restless, still disturbed by Tallent's earlier behavior in the locker room. All morning, she'd hardly been able to concentrate on taking care of patients, some of them pretty sick. It had been a real struggle.

Now with Harry, she tried to pretend everything was fine—but keeping secrets from the person she trusted most in the whole world was difficult.

"Okay, there's no sense trying to hide from me, Gina Mazzio." He reached for her hand. "What's bothering you?"

His blue eyes were always her undoing.

She couldn't stop herself, blurted out, "I think Mort Tallent intended to kill me this morning."

His mouth dropped open. "Literally kill you, right here in the hospital?"

She nodded, tried to get it together, calm herself, but she knew that wasn't going to work, not with Harry. She surrendered, let it all come out in a rush.

"I'd gone to the locker room to get something from my purse. There was no one else in the place, everyone was out on the unit. With the dim lights, it's kind of spooky in there anyway. Then Tallent popped up out of nowhere. I thought I was going to die of fright."

She forced herself to stop—to quiet down. Her heart was pounding and that trapped feeling was clawing at her chest.

"Go on," Harry said. He leaned across the Formica table. "What happened next?" He reached over, took her hand, and squeezed. "Tell me!"

"I was scared. He caught me off guard, blurted it out, 'What were you and Lolly doing in my office after hours?'"

"He's probably been waiting for an opportunity to catch you alone so he could question you."

"That wasn't it." Gina saw the concern in Harry's eyes. She wanted to stop, wipe the worry from his face, find something else to talk about. But she could see he wasn't going to allow that. "He kept moving closer and closer. There was so much venom oozing from him. I swear, if he'd had a gun, he would have shot me."

"Oh, babe, do you really think so?" Harry squeezed her hand again.

"Listen, he was beyond angry. He was crazed." She looked up and saw Vinnie and Helen making their way through the cafeteria food line.

"My brother and Helen are almost to the cashier," she said. "They'll be here in a minute or so. Please, please don't say anything. I can't stand to see Vinnie die a little bit every time something happens to me."

Harry sat back up in his seat. "You're right. We'll keep our lips zipped about any of this. Vinnie's finally getting it together. He doesn't need to know." He glanced from her to Vinnie and Helen, then back at her.

"But did Tallent actually touch you?"

"No!"

They faked interest in the cold food sitting on the table in front of them and sighed in unison as they started picking at the now unappetizing food.

Gina turned and smiled when Vinnie and Helen got to their table.

* * *

Kat Parker couldn't eat a drop of her enchilada. The melting cheese was oozing from the center of the tortilla, along with the pinto beans. Normally, she would have been fork-deep in the Mexican dish, but not today. Her appetite was gone at the thought of her cardio procedure the next morning. She couldn't stop thinking about how this could be her last day on earth. Tomorrow she might die.

But there was still time. She could call off the whole thing ... just plain chicken out.

That thought brought a sudden flood of relief—the pain in her neck disappeared and the heaviness in her chest dissipated.

Watching Cal maneuver his way to her table, tray balanced on one hand, burst that escape bubble. How could she start a new life with him and constantly worry about her health? It wouldn't be fair.

When he reached the table and sat down, she saw that they'd ordered the very same meals, from appetizer through dessert.

"Damn! We even eat alike now." He laughed and dug in, taking a mouthful of his enchilada, chewing and posing at the same time to take up another forkful. "Hey, your food's getting cold, Kat."

"I'm not very hungry today for some reason."

He looked at her. Worry lines etched his face, then deepened. "You have to eat to keep up your strength. "Please take a couple of bites. Do it for me."

She hesitated, then took a small bite. The aroma and taste made her feel a little bit better. She decided then and there that she would do what she had to do, no matter what, so she could be free to love again.

"You're really the best thing that has ever happened to me, Cal."

"I know." He gave her a big, exaggerated smile. "Now dig in before I come around there and give you a slobbery kiss right here in front of everyone., then start feeding you one bite at a time."

* * *

Vlad awakened with a start.

For a long moment he couldn't remember where he was. He tried to sit up, but pain ripped through every part of him.

He remembered Rosia had been in bed with him. He'd also heard her voice cursing him in the dark before she got up and left. When she didn't come back right away, he drifted off to sleep. Now, he carefully turned so he could see the clock on the bedside table: 12:30 p.m. He'd slept through the night and half the day.

"Hello," he semi-shouted.

No response.

"Hello, Rosia?" Again, silence.

What a stupid fool. You know she's at work now.

He scooted his legs until they hung over the edge of the bed. But he couldn't get his upper body off the mattress. It took several more tries before he managed to get into a sitting position. He sat there for awhile, painfully inhaling and exhaling as if he'd just lifted a massive weight.

When he tried to take a deep breath, steel swords jammed into his ribs. "Oh, my God!" he screamed.

You can't stay here. You need to get up and get the fuck out of here.

He finally got to his feet and swayed from side to side for a few seconds before he felt secure. Soon the room stopped spinning.

Gotta getaway from here, man.

It had taken a long time to sink in, but the pain helped him to understand.

He'd gotten too comfortable. He'd liked this identity, liked being Vlad Folo. Because of that, he hadn't relocated or changed his name in almost three years—the longest he'd ever stayed in one place, remained a single identity.

Maybe that mugging was a blessing in disguise.

He shuffled to the large full-length mirror against the wall; it took him a few seconds to get steady in front of his reflection. When he had a solid stance, he eyed his body, smothered in a crazy patchwork of bruises from bottom to top. Then he focused on his face.

"Shit!" he screamed out. He looked like he'd been run over by a train.

Nose taped, eyes a vivid purple-blue. It wasn't him. It was someone else. Someone wearing a mottled blue mask.

Disgusted, he turned around, put one foot slowly in front of the other and scuffled back to the bed.

Until he healed, he was helpless.

* * *

The tiny screen on Harry's cell showed his brother's name.

"So?" he said.

"Got you a guy, Harry. Well, actually, I got you a gal. One of the union clerks."

"She's really into computers and systems and all that shit?"

"Don't even ask me to go into it. Half the words she used were so foreign to my poor brain that I almost asked for a translator."

"Trustworthy! Is she trustworthy?"

"Oh, yeah! Know why? Don't answer. Either way, I'm gonna tell you. She thinks her mother and aunt were both bullied into surgeries they really didn't need. Her mother used up all her savings. Worse, the aunt died. This woman is ready to do most anything to yank these kinds of doctors out of hiding, expose any treatment that's not on the up and up."

"She wasn't worried about the legal implications?" Harry said.

"We discussed that in the beginning. She was a little hesitant at first, said what you really needed was a 'black hat' hacker.' You know, someone who's into it for personal gain, or is just plain malicious."

"Well, that's not us."

"Maybe not, but that's the kind of hacker you need. She calls herself a 'white hat.' Helps people test their security systems ... retrieves lost passwords for friends ... that sort of thing."

"But will she help?"

"Yes. She's even excited about it."

"When can Gina and I get together with her?"

"I've got her phone number. She'll be expecting a call from you."

Chapter 38

Gina dropped Harry off right after work, gave him a wave, and drove off. He stood in the rain for a moment and watched the back of her beloved, cranky Fiat roadster as she drove away.

It is kinda cute.

He wondered again if she'd ever give up on that funky car. Knew she'd probably always find a way to breathe life back into it, if it took her own dying breath.

Harry climbed up the stairs and stood at Paul's door, waiting for his older brother to answer his knock. Sooner or later he would open up, if for no other reason than to yell, "Go away!"

That was their ritual.

Harry was always hesitant to use the key Paul had given him the day his brother moved in to this bachelor's apartment after a contentious divorce. That day he'd insisted that Harry take the key. "I need to know there's someone out there who cares whether I'm alive or dead."

That was more than two years ago.

It was probably that memory more than anything else that kept Harry from using the key—he was always afraid that one day he would unlock the door and find Paul dead.

It had been a really sad time. Even now, Paul still tried to get his ex-wife, now re-married, to change her mind and take him back. His brother couldn't let it go.

Harry thought of Gina and realized how many times they'd come close to losing each other, too.

The Lucke men never seem to give up, no matter what. Like wolves, we mate for life.

Paul always acted annoyed when he had to answer the door, but Harry was never sure whether it was a façade to discourage unwanted guests, or real. And Harry didn't like barging in on anyone, not even his brother.

Live and let live.

That reason alone made him uncomfortable with the idea that they were going to hack into someone's computer and romp through supposedly confidential information.

Cyberspace didn't seem real to Harry—maybe most people felt the same way. He didn't know for sure, but he suspected that it was true. Virtual reality wasn't something you could define easily and it definitely wasn't touchable.

That was the *virtual* part.

When he thought about the nebulous iCloud holding all the information on the planet, it made his eyes cross. Mostly, you just had to accept, like quantum physics, that it really did exist, even if you didn't know what the hell it was.

If there was a place that held all the world's important information, he was about to use it to abandon his own ethics and violate someone's right to privacy.

His brother flung open the door. "Again! What's with not using your key?"

"I hate doing it." Harry walked into the apartment and noticed that even after the big cleanup, the place was already morphing into Paul's usual messy man-cave.

His brother ambled into the kitchen and pulled a beer out of the refrigerator and gave it to him. Harry sprawled out on the sofa.

"So is all of this real?" Harry took a long pull from the bottle. "Did you really find someone to help us?"

"Yeah, it's the woman I mentioned to you yesterday. Hell, you spoke to her on the phone." Paul looked at his watch. "She should be here any time now."

"What's she like?"

"Are you kidding me, little brother? What are you expecting?"

"I don't know. Knowing you, it could be someone covered with tats and sporting a lot of face jewelry." Harry laughed at the look on his brother's disbelieving face. "Oh, come on, Paul. I'm pulling your leg. I don't know what to expect."

"Well, she works in the union office around a lot of big bruisers, so you know she can take care of herself."

The door bell rang with an impatient dot...dot sound.

"You can see for yourself." Paul set his beer bottle on the coffee table and jumped up to open the front door. An attractive woman, somewhere in her early thirties, with an inquisitive tilt to her head, stepped inside. Her hair was drenched, as was the coat she was wearing.

"Sheesh, is it ever gonna stop raining?"

Paul took her coat, hung it on a hall closet door knob where it dripped water on the floor.

"Christina, this is my brother, Harry."

She reached out and shook Harry's hand, held onto for a long moment while she scrutinized his face. He was certain that whatever vibrations she got from her brief once-over would have a lot to do with her decision as to whether she would work with them.

After a moment, Christina smiled, dropped his hand, plopped down next to him on the sofa. "How about a beer, Paul?" She turned to Harry. "I hear you're a nurse?"

"Guilty, as charged," Harry said, smiling.

"What kind of nursing do you do?"

"I'm usually a travel nurse. You know, I work on contract for whoever needs me, most anywhere in the States. Right now, I'm working here at Ridgewood in ICU."

"Mmmm, my instincts tell me," she said seriously, studying his face, "you're top notch."

Harry didn't realize just how tense he was until a long breath escaped his lips.

* * *

They'd been making small talk, eating a home-delivered pizza, and drinking beer for almost an hour when Christina said, "Okay, tell me exactly why you want into this guy's files, Harry? I mean, it's a challenge and fun, but also damn risky ... and as illegal as a physical B&E."

"Mainly, we're sure this doctor has been cooking his books—not reporting income, which is really none of our business. But, we're fairly certain that in the process of lining his pockets, he's also performing unnecessary patient procedures."

"Yeah, well, I think doctors do that all the time, but they usually don't get into trouble for it." Tears suddenly filled her eyes. "My aunt died because she was pushed into an unnecessary surgery." She sniffed, reached into her purse for a tissue, and blew her nose. "Couldn't prove it, of course, even though I tried."

"Yeah," Harry said, "malpractice isn't easy to prove ... insurance companies make sure of that."

"Tell me more," Christina said.

Paul went back into the kitchen, asked if anyone wanted another beer.

"Not me," Harry said.

"Christina?"

"Sure, why not?"

"Since unnecessary surgeries are hard to prove" Harry said, "we're more interested in outing him for padding Medicare charges for procedures, and cheating insurance companies."

Christina gave him a squint. There was speculation in her eyes and her faint frown lines deepened.

"You're not giving me the whole story, are you Harry? Like, there's something more going on here."

"No, no! This is what we need to know."

"Yeah, sure. And what else?" Christina took a long pull on her beer bottle. "I don't dig that you're doing this just to protect the government or insurance companies from being ripped off." She shook her head from side to side. "Nope, I just don't buy it."

Harry stared into her eyes. "You might not want to hear the rest of it." Harry picked up another piece of pizza and tentatively took a bite.

"Look, man, you know where I work ... and what Paul does for a living." She took another long pull from her beer bottle. "I won't tell you where the dead bodies are buried, but I've got to know why I'm jumping into this, or I'm out. What you've told me here, well—"

"—okay! Okay!" Harry said. "This doctor, along with everything else I've said, is involved in murder. We're sure of it. Maybe more than one." Harry leaned over, his face, up close. "Do you really want to know more?"

Bette Golden Lamb & J. J. Lamb

Chapter 39

Kat was terrified. She hung onto Cal's arm as he drove her to Dr. Tallent's office.

"You don't have to go inside with me," she said, not wanting to let go of him. "I'm okay now. Really, I am."

But she wasn't. She was spinning out of control and he was her anchor, her only anchor.

"You don't get it, do you, Kat?"

She looked at him, wanting him to turn around and take her home.

"I'm not leaving you. Do you understand? We're doing this together."

When they walked into the waiting room, instead of the receptionist, a nurse in blue scrubs was waiting at the side of the desk. She smiled and motioned to Kat.

"Hi," the nurse said. "Are you Kathryn Parker?"

"Yes, that's me."

"Great. I'm Dara." She held out a hand. "Can I see your identification, please?"

Kat fumbled through her purse and handed the nurse her driver's license. The nurse checked it carefully, then looked at Kat and compared her face to the DMV photo before returning the license.

The nurse reached for her hand. "Let's ID you for the procedure, Kathryn."

"Call me Kat, please."

She held out her arm and the nurse wrapped a plastic identification bracelet around her wrist. It showed her name, Tallent's name, and her A negative blood type.

"I'm going to take you into the pre-op holding area and we'll get you ready for your procedure."

181

Kat thought her heart would fly right out of her chest. "Can Cal come in with me?"

"I'm sorry, Kat, but he'll have to wait for you out here."

She turned to him. For a single moment, she thought about grabbing his hand and running—running far away.

He came to her, took her in his arms, then held her at arm's length and gave her a reassuring smile. "I'll be right here waiting for you."

She nodded and stepped away. The nurse kept the door open. Kat stopped, turned, and took one more look at Cal. She made her shaking fingers wave goodbye before following the nurse down the hallway.

"When was the last time you had something to eat?"

"About ten last night."

"Good," the nurse said. "I'm sure Dr. Tallent explained the procedure, but I'll go over it again for you after you're changed."

Kat followed the nurse into a small room with a bench and two lockers—both doors were open. "Go ahead and undress, then put your clothes and purse inside one of the lockers. It's secured by your own four-number pin." She handed Kat a blue paper gown. "Opening's in the back, of course. I'll give you a few minutes to get ready."

When she was ready, she leaned against one wall and started to cry.

I finally get my life together and now ... this.

The nurse returned, took one look at Kat and wrapped her arms around her. "It's going to be all right."

"How do you know that?" Kat said, choking up and swallowing her words. "I could die on that table."

Kat dropped down onto the bench; the nurse sat down beside her. "Look, we do these all the time. Yes, things can go wrong ... I'm sure Dr. Tallent talked to you about that. But the chances of that happening are very, very small. "

"We're talking about me, so if anything can go wrong, it will."

The nurse took her hand and they walked a short distance to the pre-op holding area. "Now, let's s get you down on this table and in a few minutes I'll give you some meds to help you relax."

Flat on her back, Kat stared at the ceiling and started shaking.

The nurse covered her with a warm blanket. "This will make you more comfortable."

It did make her feel better. She started to relax. "Thank you."

The nurse stepped up to a computer station, hit a few keys, and smiled. "I see you're not on many medications. Are you allergic to anything—meds, foods. Anything at all?"

"No."

Dr. Tallent walked into the room, without knocking. "She should be ready by now, Dara. Let's get a move on." Almost as an after though, he said, "How are you doing, Kat?"

Before she could answer, he was out the door.

The nurse's face flushed. Kat turned away. "I'm going to start your IV. This will hurt for a moment," Dara said.

The needle did hurt. She tried to take deep breaths.

"Will I be completely out?"

"No, but you really won't care about what's going on." The nurse laughed and taped down the needle. "We're really good at that."

Kat watched the nurse inject medication into an IV port— almost instantly she felt a sense of relaxation.

* * *

Mort Tallent hardly slept the night before. He'd tossed and turned, angry at Vlad Folo's silence. Lately, he couldn't get rid of the guy, but now that he wanted to talk to him, had left several messages; there wasn't a peep out of him.

Tallent had decided—Vlad would have to get rid of Gina Mazzio. He knew if he didn't, sooner or later she was going to go to the police. That nurse was not only nosey, she had a big mouth. It was stupid to confront her in that locker room at Ridgewood. Almost lost it—could have choked the life out of her.

Don't know what the fuck came over me. I should have left her alone. Let the gladiator get her off my back. Cough up the lousy fifty grand and stay out of the arena.

He scrubbed in and watched the final preparations through the glass window that separated him from the Cardio Cath Lab.

The nurse was doing a final check of the equipment, together with a specialist from X-Ray. The scrub nurse was arranging things on the sterile field, making sure all the necessary equipment was ready.

Focus, man. Focus!

* * *

Kat kept floating in and out. Her eyes fluttered to stay open and she heard every word, every sound.

The doctor said something about a sheath of some kind, and how they had to thread the catheter into her artery. Words floated around and away ... blood thinners ... contrast dye ... warm feeling ... angiogram ... flow measurement ... coronary arteries ... no narrowing ... no blockage. The words just ebbed and flowed without having any real meaning.

* * *

At first Tallent's head was where it was supposed to be. He was focused—numbing the groin area, placing the sheath into the femoral artery, guiding the catheter to the heart with the aid of the fluoroscope, but after that his mind started wandering. A roar of pounding waves surged through his head—he was riding the big surf, down under a massive curl. He was hot, getting dizzy.

"Doctor, are you all right?"

"Yes! I'm fine! Let's get on with it."

I can get through this. There's nothing wrong here. I have to focus. Focus!

But the roar of the surf was shutting out everything around him. He couldn't hear, couldn't think.

Bette Golden Lamb & J. J. Lamb

Chapter 40

Cal had been in and out of his chair for the past three hours. He couldn't relax. He'd pick up a magazine, thumb through it for a few minutes, toss it back on the table, get up and pace some more.

What the hell's taking so long?

More and more people came into the reception room; no one seemed to leave. All of the new arrivals were hesitant, appeared nervous and restless. None of it did anything to improve Cal's mood. At first it had just been him—now there were several people doing the same magazine-pace-magazine-pace thing.

He looked at the door to the inner sanctum. Kat couldn't be all that far away, but she might as well be on another continent, another planet.

He closed his eyes, tried to close his mind to everything except good thoughts about Kat. He hadn't known her all that long, but what he did know, he loved. She was good-natured, kind, and when they were together, she made him laugh, see a different world.

A better world.

He'd been divorced a long time and most of the women he'd met were far too involved in petty, useless interests. That, or desperate to find someone to hook up with. Kat wasn't like that. She was a little older than the women he'd dated recently, but when people talked to her, she listened.

She cared.

He wasn't used to walking down the streets handing out money to almost every indigent person who came up to them.

"You know, they'll only spend it on booze," he'd said the first time she gave money to a panhandler.

"I hear that a lot, Cal. But when I give money to someone, it's not mine anymore. They'll do whatever they have to do. It's really not my business."

At first it irritated him, but he began to understand. She wasn't there to judge—just to help.

* * *

Kat heard the nursing staff talking and moving about her—they weren't paying attention to her and she knew that was probably a good thing.

Happiness washed over her, along with gratitude. She was still alive.

It must be over. I'm still here!

Her right leg felt weird, though. It was numb and a sudden, strange sensation made her want to jump.

"Dara!" she called out. "There's something wrong with my leg."

The nurse came across the room, smiling. "Hi, glad to see you're back to reality."

"There's something wrong. It's my leg."

The nurse, continuing to smile, lifted the light blanket covering Kat's lower body. She removed a dressing and the smile faded.

"Do you feel that?" the nurse asked, touching her leg.

Kat couldn't feel anything.

"Close your eyes and rest, Kat. I'm going to get in touch with Dr. Tallent and we'll see what he has to say."

"What's wrong with my leg?"

"Try to rest. I'll be right back."

Kat could see Dara speaking on the telephone, asking for Dr. Tallent.

"What do you mean he's signed out?" The nurse sounded both annoyed and scared.

Kat's heart was galloping.

"Okay, then please get me Dr. Cantor. Now!"

"Yes, yes, I understand. Don't bother him if he's in surgery."

The nurse came back to her. "Kat, Dr Tallent isn't available right now, so I'm. going to get Dr. Brichett. He's here in the office seeing patients. We'll get him out here to check your leg. Okay?"

"What's wrong with my leg?"

"It may be nothing, but I think one of the doctors should take a look. Okay?"

Kat couldn't speak. Why wasn't Dara answering her question? She closed her eyes and tried to ignore the strange feeling in her leg.

* * *

Jon Brichett was about to walk into an examination room when Dara came running down the hall, her face was red. She looked frightened.

"Jon, wait! I need you to check one of Mort's post-op patients."

"What do you mean? For God's sake, where's Mort?"

"I don't know. I can't reach him anywhere."

Brichett was stunned. He'd been having such a good day, but a tickle at the base of his neck turned into an alarm. If Dara wanted him to check something, it needed to be checked.

"You've paged him?"

"Of course I paged him."

"What's the problem?"

"I think there's an occlusion in her femoral. Her leg is cold. I tried for a distal pulse."

"And?"

"Negative. No pulse. She's alternating between pain and paresthesia. Used the Doppler—nothing."

"Okay! Let's go!"

They'd only gone a couple of steps when he stopped at a wall phone and pushed a button for the receptionist.

"Hi! Please reschedule the patient in Room One. Make certain he gets another appointment as soon as possible." He started to hang up, then added, "And cancel the rest of my morning."

The moment they walked into post-op, one of the other nurses said, "I still can't reach Mort Tallent."

Brichett turned to Dara. "What's the patient's name and how long has she been post-op?"

Dara's eyes were wide with worry. "Kat Parker. I have her history already up on the monitor for you. She's about an hour post op."

"And Tallent's gone already? Shit!"

Brichett scanned Kat's chart, turned, and hurried into the recovery room. There were two women on gurneys, but it took only one glance to tell which one was Kat Parker—her face had that look of terror he'd seen on more patients than he cared to remember.

"Hi, Ms. Parker. I'm Dr. Brichett, one of Dr. Tallent's associates. They tell me your leg is giving you problems. I'd like to take a look, okay?"

She bit her lower her lip and nodded.

Brichett turned the sheet aside and looked at the bone-white leg. Moving to her ankle, he felt around for a pulse. There was none.

"Where's Dr. Tallent?" Kat said, her voice barely audible.

"He's been ... uh ... been called away . But I promise, we'll take good care of you."

"What's the matter with me?"

"Did the person who brought you here stay?"

"Yes. He's my boyfriend, Cal Cortez. He's in the waiting room."

"Do you want him to be with you?"

The patient nodded again.

"Dara, please get Mr. Cortez and bring him here so he can be with Ms. Parker."

* * *

Cal had started a new pacing cycle when the same nurse he'd seen earlier came rushing through the door."

"Mr. Cortez, please come with me. Ms. Parker asked to speak to you."

His heart boomed in his chest. "What's wrong? Is something wrong with Kat?"

"There's been a problem. Dr. Brichett will explain it to you."

The nurse's voice was soft and kind but he imagined the worst as he followed her to the recovery room. The smells in the hallway brought a moment of *déjà vu*—he was back in the hospital where he'd been taken with a ruptured appendix many years ago. It took him a moment to realize someone was speaking to him.

"Hi, Mr. Cortez. I'm Dr. Brichett. Sorry to meet under these circumstances."

Cal nodded and looked down at Kat, who looked back with tear-filled eyes. He moved to her side, grabbed onto her hand, and squeezed. "Hi, kiddo. Am I ever happy to see you."

On the other side of the gurney, Brichett said, "Kat, we're going to have to take you over to Ridgewood Hospital. It doesn't happen often, but sometimes after a Cardio Cath a clot develops in the artery that supplies the blood to your leg. That's what's happened here and we need to take care of it. Right away."

Both Kat and Cal were crying.

"We're calling for an ambulance." Brichett nodded at the nurse and she hurried out of the room.

"What's going to happen to my leg?" Kat shouted. "Am I going to lose my leg?"

Shivers ran up and down Cal's spine.

Chapter 41

Mort Tallent raced into the Time Out Health Club. Rosia, as usual, was sitting at the desk with her breasts half out of her scoop-neck blouse. A big smile was plastered across her face.

"Good morning, Dr. Tallent. How nice to see you again."

Tallent's stomach churned, his head was swimming in pain. He wanted to punch her in the face, rip that stupid blouse from her body.

He jammed his hands in his pocket.

"I have to see Vlad," he said with a forced a smile. "I have a ... a terrible headache. He's the best at getting rid of them."

"Vlad is out, doctor," she said in that maddening saccharin voice she affected. "But we have other experts who can help you equally as well."

"No. No one is as good as Vlad."

"I'm so sorry, doctor, but Vlad has been out for a few days recovering from an accident. He won't be in for several more days."

What the fuck am I going to do now?

"Is there any way I can reach him?" Tallent said. "It's really important."

Rosia leaned over the counter and Tallent had no choice but to look down into the deep cleavage that was now only inches from his face. "There's a teensy-weensy chance I might be able to get a message to him."

"I'd rather talk to him in person."

Rosia straightened up, the wide smile vanishing to only a slight upturn at the corners of her mouth. "I'll bet you would, doctor, but I'm afraid that's impossible."

Tallent wanted to scream at her—his stomach was a roiling volcano and the roaring in his ears had started again.

"Could I write a note to him and maybe you'll see that he gets it as soon as possible?"

"Oh, I can try," Rosia said. "But I can't guarantee anything."

Tallent pulled out his wallet and removed a $100 bill. He folded the bill twice and slipped it under the edge of her appointment book, the same as he'd done previously when he'd needed a favor.

"Maybe that will cover the cost of your finding him," he said.

The cleavage retreated and quickly became the repository for the folded bill.

"Yes, it will." She pulled out a pad from the desk and passed it across to him. "Do you need a pen, Dr. Tallent?"

Stupid cow.

"No, no. I have my own."

He sat down in a small waiting area for customers, picked up a body building magazine to use for support, and glanced briefly at the steroid-happy bodies pictured on the front. With a snort, he covered up a muscle-bound man and wrote a cryptic message:

> Vlad,
>> I need you to permanently take care of that nurse situation we recently discussed.
>> Please get in touch with me as soon as possible.
>>> -M.T

* * *

Alex had been sitting in his car the past two days waiting for this Vlad person to show up.

He wanted to get a good look at this man. He'd never seen him as a kid because twenty years ago their Russian gang only dealt with the parents.

Why wasn't the boy with his mother and father that day when he and his stupid partner went to that hovel of an apartment?

Alexander had gone over that day in his mind a thousand times.

After killing the couple, they'd left the apartment and waited in the car for the boy to come home. He never arrived.

How could that miserable couple have warned the kid to stay away when Alex and Misha had caught the two of them completely off-guard? The only answer: the boy *was* in the apartment that day, hidden so they wouldn't find him.

Alex couldn't understand. How could any child watch or hear the slaughter he and Misha carried out and remain silent?

Around noon, his stomach started growling like a beast.

Idiot! Should have packed some food.

He decided to go someplace nearby, eat, come back to wait. Hope that miserable Vlad did not arrive in the meantime.

Chapter 42

Gina was just back from an early lunch when Gwen, the CCU team leader caught her walking down the hall.

"Gina, I'm going to need you to scrub in with Jon Brichett. Immediately!"

"Yeah, sure. What's up?"

The team leader was flustered. "An emergency thrombectomy ... post-op Cardio Cath ."

"Brichett must be upset. That kind of thing doesn't happen to him, at least not very often."

"He's more like pissed ... she's one of Mort Tallent's patients."

"Why is Brichett doing the surgery if it's Tallent's patient?"

"No one gave me the scoop on that," Gwen said. "All I know is, the ambulance will be here any minute ... and the clock is ticking. The patient has had negative leg and pedal pulses for almost two hours."

"Jeez, she must have been on anticoagulants. Shouldn't that have taken care of the clots in the OR?"

"Tell that to the gods."

Gina hurried to the CCU emergency OR and started pulling packs of wrapped sterile set-ups. She opened the outer layers, then rushed out to the scrub area, masked up, and started brushing hard at her nails, hands, and arms. Pretty soon she was joined by Brichett.

"Thought I'd be eating lunch by now," he said. "My stomach's growling like a trapped bear."

"What's up with Mort?" Gina had reached her arms and was scrubbing hard at the skin. "This is his patient, right?"

Even with his mask on, Gina could see the irritation in Brichett's eyes when he turned to her. "Let's just say, there's trouble in Oz these days."

Gina couldn't let it go. "He really gave my friend Lolly a bad time."

"We were sorry to lose her," Brichett said. "Lolly was a great nurse. I don't know what happened, but she just up and left. She must have been spooked by something; that's what it looked like to me. Hope it wasn't the result of something Tallent did."

I don't know yet. But I'm going to find out.

Gina turned away from the sink. "Think I better get moving."

* * *

Kat was inconsolable. Even with the medications they'd given her, she was anxious and couldn't get past the idea that she might lose her leg. She clutched Cal's hand in the ambulance.

"Please try to relax." He leaned over and kissed her. "It's going to be all right, Kat. You'll see."

"But what if I lose my leg?"

"Whatever happens, we'll deal with it," he said, "but Dr. Brichett thinks you're going to be fine."

"But where's Dr. Tallent?" she said. "He's my doctor. Nobody seems to know where he is."

"Dr. Brichett is his partner. I'm sure he'll take good care of you."

The medication was starting to kick in. She looked at Cal and could swear there was an aura of light around him. All her worry and pain took a step back.

She closed her eyes and said, "I love you, Cal. I really do love you."

* * *

By the time Jon Brichett finished scrubbing and walked into the OR, Gina had set up for an arterial thrombectomy. He couldn't

198

help feeling uneasy knowing what the patient had at stake. He would do his best and hope the fates were on their side.

Brichett watched as Kathryn Parker was lifted from the gurney to the table with a steadying sheet underneath to keep her from changing position. He needed her as still as possible.

"Let's see if we can get by without a general," he said.

The anesthesiologist nodded and started the IV meds for conscious sedation.

"Hopefully, this will be quick," Brichett said.

"Her leg is white as snow," Gina said.

"Still no pedal pulse," said the circulating nurse.

Brichett nodded. "Let's just do what we have to do and get blood flowing to that leg."

To Brichett, it seemed like no time between incision and placement of the Fogarty catheter that stabilized and withdrew thrombus material from the proximal and distal segments of the femoral artery.

"And?" Brichett said to the circulating nurse, holding his breath.

It seemed to take forever until the nurse smiled. "Pinking up."

Everyone in the room let out a collective, "Whoa!"

* * *

Cal was in the waiting room, hyperventilating and dizzy. He hadn't stopped pacing since the door closed behind Kat. He couldn't remember the last time he'd been this frightened.

He and Kat had just found each other and now he might lose her. He tried to sit down jumped back up, looked around the room helplessly, and started pacing again.

When the door opened, he spun around, stopped, and watched the Dr Brichett come into the waiting room, head in his direction with a smile on his face.

Cal covered his face and sobbed.

Bette Golden Lamb & J. J. Lamb

Chapter 43

Mort Tallent thought everything had gone well with Kat Parker's procedure ... until the final moments. There was something about the way the catheter hung up at one point that set off an alarm in his head.

No! Got to get out of here. Now! Run!

"Suture her. Finish her up," he said to his assistant.

He rushed out of the OR to the locker room, stepped out of his scrubs, and all but ran out of the unit.

Hurrying along the hallways, he took the elevator down to the underground parking garage. As soon as he was in his car and hit the ignition, he accelerated out of the building, tires screeching.

Once on the street, he turned off his cell, and took a deep breath. Finally, he could breathe again.

The rain was coming down hard. The sound of it beating on his windshield, along with the slosh and song of the water under his tires began to calm him.

Have to get away. Can't stand this anymore.

He could leave his practice behind ... as soon as he knew Gina Mazzio was taken out. *She* knew what was going on. *She* was the danger. *She* was the only obstacle standing between him and freedom.

Freedom! A word he hadn't thought of for many years.

Lolly and Gina.

Nosy nurses who just couldn't stay out of his business, had to sneak into his computer, try to ruin his life. Well, that wasn't going to happen.

He drove around the city aimlessly after he left a message for Vlad at the health club. Then he headed toward Half Moon Bay. With each mile that pushed San Francisco farther behind him, he could feel the tension in his neck easing.

He finally pulled into a parking lot near the ocean and got out of the car. He took off his shoes and walked slowly down to the beach. The rain was like sheets of ice water drenching him, but it also cleansed him and made him feel whole.

He walked back and forth along the water's edge. The sound of the rain and the crashing waves created peace deep inside. He looked around and saw he was surrounded by absolute emptiness. There wasn't anyone or anything else within sight as the massive waves rolled toward the shore, crashing onto the rocks, smashing into the shoreline.

He screamed, "Freedom."

His mind was clear again. Everything in its proper place.

He would finish Gina Mazzio, finish the week's procedures, finish his life in San Francisco, and leave.

* * *

Jon Brichett was flipping angry. No! He wasn't angry, he was freaking mad.

What the hell happened to Mort? Walking out, disappearing on a post–op patient like that.

Unbelievable! The man's unraveling right before our eyes.

Brichett tried Tallent's telephone number again. He called the exchange that handled their calls. Nothing.

Damn it!

Kat Parker was one lucky woman. It gave him a certain pleasure to know that he'd saved her leg.

No thanks to that fucker Tallent

It always amazed him how tough, yet how fragile the human body was. Working in these dire situations always left him with more questions than answers.

Were all the dangers, the hazards that humans endured, acts of vengeful gods? Or were they only the random acts of a disinterested universe?

He'd stopped trying to figure it out years ago. Now he only tried to do the very best he could every single day.

* * *

It was late when Tallent walked into the offices. He headed straight for the post-op holding area.

The rooms were empty. His heart raced at the thought that the worst might have happened. Something had definitely gone wrong. There were no post-op patients—they were all discharged.

Kat Parker should have been there with the nurses, awaiting his further orders.

He went to his office, turned on the lights, and was startled to see Jon Brichett sitting in the chair opposite his desk. Brichett looked wasted.

"You son-of-a-bitch!" Brichett said with menace. "Where the hell have you been?"

Tallent, soaking wet, collapsed into his desk chair and looked across at the fuming Brichett, normally the best-humored of the three doctors in the three-man practice. "I'm sorry, Jon. I had to leave."

"Just walk out without telling anyone—without having someone cover your patient? Are you insane?" Brichett leaned forward. "Kat Parker almost lost her leg. She could have died."

"She was fine when I left."

"You're a liar," Brichett screamed at him. "I back-tracked this. You have no idea what kind of condition she was in. You just walked away. Left the Parker woman high and dry."

"Is she all right?"

"No thanks to you, you fucking bastard. Thanks to people more caring than you, she still has two legs to walk on."

Tallent covered his face with both hands. His whole body shook.

"What's going on?" Cantor asked, his head sticking into Tallent's office, one hand on the doorframe. "I could hear you shouting all the way down the hall, Jon."

Brichett turned to face Cantor. "Our friend here decided to finally come back and check on the mess he left behind."

"What happened to you?" Cantor demanded of Tallent.

Tallent looked at his two partners, knew he should feel some kind of warmth toward these men, with whom he'd share a practice for many years. He felt nothing ... nothing other than an urge to stand and run from the office.

"You know things have been difficult for me since Annie died. Well, it's become too much. I've decided to leave the practice in a week or two, or as soon as I can get everything tidied up. I think it's best for all of us."

Cantor and Brichett looked at each other.

"You're going to walk out on us with only a week or two notice?" Cantor snapped. "That's it?"

Brichett sat in his chair, looking at Tallent and shaking his head.

"Yes, that's it." Tallent slipped out of his wet jacket and laid it across the top of his desk, ignoring the papers underneath that were absorbing the moisture.

"Mort, at least give us six months," Brichett said. "We need some time to conduct interviews and find someone who might fit into the practice."

"That's not going to happen," Tallent said.

He stood and snatched up his jacket, scattering papers everywhere. He gave a curt nod to Brichett, pushed past Cantor, and walked out.

Chapter 44

Alex sat in his car most of the day, watching, waiting for the man he had to kill. He thought about those years—time lost chasing shadows, wanting to leave and return to his homeland, his wife and children—living on the dribbles of money his people doled out to him.

An empty life bound by his gang's obsession to kill one meaningless person—the man who was once a boy, and Alex had to kill him.

Why did it matter after all this time?

It was the code. The fucking code that even required proof that he had killed the boy/man.

He read American magazines, looked at streaming movies on his laptop, and studied pictures of his grown children. He thought about the things that were once his—pictures all flashing before him on the small computer screen.

During the past twenty years, he'd spent searching for the son of Nadya and Ivan Antonev, he'd lost any sense of what had been his real life—a life he'd loved and left behind in Russia. There, he'd been someone who had all the money he needed, had real opportunities in the organization. The head man liked him; the people he worked with liked him.

All that changed the day he didn't find and kill Dimitri Antonev, who became, Karl Pushkin, and now, he was sure was Vlad Folo.

Dimitri's parents had double-crossed the Russian Mafia, refused to continue to store the gang's illegal narcotics in their warehouse. The Antonevs had taken one, fatal step that had sealed their doom—they stole and sold the last shipment of drugs to finance their escape from Russia and live fugitive lives in America.

Bette Golden Lamb & J. J. Lamb

A death warrant had been issued and Alexander was put in charge of finding and carrying out the family's death sentence.

When he failed to kill the boy, he'd been given a choice: find the boy or forfeit his own life. That was his only choice.

Alex had a family to support in Minsk. How much time could it take to find a Russian boy alone on the streets? A boy with no family, no connections should have been an easy snatch.

He'd been wrong. He'd had no idea of how large the San Francisco Bay Area was, or how many run-aways roamed and survived in the streets.

Over the years, he'd paid and found out information about a hit man that Alex suspected had to be the boy. At times he was right on his heels—the kid managed to escape every time. The hit man may have started out as a boy, but he turned into a man. A man who had learned to change his identity, his address, and become the mist in the morning dew that disappeared in the heat of the sun.

Alex was forced to do menial jobs for the Russian mob, not only in San Francisco, but also New York while he continued to search for Dimitri Antonev/Karl Pushkin. But there still was no retreat from the decision—he could not return home until the matter was settled.

One year, two years ... twenty years disappeared while he sought to redeem himself and follow the shadow of the boy.

* * *

It was four p.m. and Vlad, the suspected Antonev son, had not been to the health club.

Alex watched the receptionist step out of the building, leave for the day.

What was her name?

Saw the name tag pinned on that ample bosom of hers when I made the appointment for a massage.

206

He closed his eyes, pressed the heels of his hands against his temples, and tried to close out every other thought, every nearby noise.

Rosia! Da, that's it! Rosia..

He opened his eyes just as she started down the sidewalk. He continued to watch her walk straight as an arrow, in high stiletto heels, swaying her ample hips. In the middle of the block, she got in the driver's side of a gleaming black, late-model Chrysler 300.

When the car pulled away from the curb, Alex, on a hunch, pulled out and followed.

* * *

Rosia was feeling pretty smug. She'd snapped up an extra C-note today and all she had to do was deliver a dumb message to Vlad from a man in a cheap suit that made appointments for body work with Vlad.

At least Vlad was good for something.

hat an idiot she'd been to pick him up that night—a beaten down, penniless, whipped puppy.

All she ever wanted was to be with strong men who would take care of her, but she always seemed to end up with loser after loser. Not that Vlad ever wanted her—he'd made that pretty plain the first time she came on to him. Right now, she couldn't remember what she'd ever seen in him. He was very ugly now.

Stupid man!

She'd wanted to take him to a doctor when he was all broken up with his smashed nose. But he refused—said she'd done a good enough job on him. Well, maybe so, but that banged up nose of his wasn't going to improve with this last beating just by her tape job.

And those scars all over his back. My God! Wouldn't talk about them. Said it was none of my fuckin' business. Sponges off of me and it's none of my business? What a mess!

Helluva way to treat someone who saved your ass.

She walked into the apartment, expected Vlad to be asleep, but there he was doing push-ups in the living room in his underwear—the same shorts she'd had to go buy at the thrift shop after he refused to let her go to his apartment to get his clothes.

"Well, well, here you are, up and around. You must be feeling more like yourself. It's about time."

He ignored her and kept on with his pathetic exercise routine, which pissed her off even more.

"I see the place is still a mess," she said, looking at the kitchen, where his dirty dishes were strewn around the sink and table, like he expected some maid to come in and clean up after him.

"Hey, you! Vlad! I'm talking to you."

He moved like lightning, up from the floor, hands encircling her neck. "Listen, bitch! Don't you ever talk to me like that again. You hear me?"

She nodded, her head moving like a bobble doll.

After he released her, she looked into his eyes. There was nothing there. Not even hatred.

Rosia glared at him, rubbed her neck, and hissed, "I have a note for you."

* * *

Vlad found the pain irritating as he forced himself to work out. He knew he had to exercise. His ribs obviously had been badly bruised, although not cracked, in the beating because they started healing right away, like the rest of him.

In the past few days, he'd begun to improve rapidly, especially after he started staying under the hot shower until there was only cold water coming out of the shower head. Then he forced himself to remain under the icy spray until he was shaking. He disliked it intensely, but he could feel himself growing stronger, almost by the hour.

When he read Tallent's note, he knew things would start going his way again. He would kill the nurse and make another easy fifty grand.

Vlad now accepted the signs, the ones that warned him it was time for a new identity and a new place to live. He'd been Vlad Folo for too many years. He could almost feel the dragon's breath of a stalker burning his neck.

The last time it happened, someone crashed in his door. He was out the window and down the fire escape in an instant. There'd been signs then, but he'd been comfortable then, too.

Slow to react—almost too slow.

* * *

"What are you making for diner?" Vlad asked Rosia. He was dressed in grubby clothes, more of what she'd gotten for him at the thrift shop. "I'm hungry."

She wanted to hit him up alongside the head, but those dead eyes of his made her hold back. When he turned away from her in disgust, she grabbed a steak knife from the counter and slipped it into her pocket.

"I don't have enough money to feed both you and me." Rosia fought to keep her voice even. "We've gone through all my pantry supplies and I'm broke." She gave him a nasty look. "We both know you haven't contributed a cent, so I guess its soup for dinner."

His stride was strong again and in two long steps he was at her purse, rummaged in it until he found her wallet. He pulled out the C-note, then also peeled off several more bills, the smallest a ten.

"You bitch!" He pocketed the money.

She tried to calm herself, but she was scared. "Look, Vlad, I was happy to help you out, but I think it's time you left. You're strong now and I can't afford to have a ... an extra person hanging on." She tried to soften her words with a smile.

He pulled a magnet off the refrigerator that advertised a local pizza delivery joint, tossed it to her. "Order two large ones with everything."

"You've got all my money. You'll have to pay for it."

He opened the freezer door and pulled out packet after packet of frozen cash.

"I think you can afford it."

He looked at her stunned expression and hated her. He knew the only reason Rosia picked him up that horrible night when he was beaten and down was in the hope she could get money out of him.

Didn't work out that way, did it, little Rosia? Instead I've got your three thousand dollars.

Her eyes were wide with terror and her blouse dipped down over those big boobs. He felt a stirring in his groin. He'd never thought of her as someone to have sex with, but now he wanted to see what was under her clothes.

He started stripping his pants off. "Get undressed."

"No, Vlad! I've been working all day. I'm too—"

"—did you hear what I said, bitch?"

"Come on..."

Her resistance was making him hard. He'd only wanted to intimidate her, but her fear, the smell of her sweat, was making his blood stir.

"Did you hear what I said, Rosia? Did you?"

She was watching him grow—she stepped back, pulled the a puny kitchen knife out of her pocket and held it out in front of her.

He laughed, pulled off his shirt, and stood naked before her. He was pleased the bruises that had covered most of his body had faded to yellow and he knew in a couple of days they would be gone.

Her hand was shaking as he grabbed her wrist; the knife fell to the floor. He twisted her arm almost to the point of breaking, stopped when she cried out in pain.

"Please don't hurt me anymore!"

He picked up the knife, bounced it in the palm of his hand. "This is the best you could do to defend yourself? You're pitiful."

"I'm sorry, Vlad. You were scaring me."

He grabbed her around the waist, lifted her, carried her to the counter, sat her on the edge with her legs spread apart.

"Open yourself!"

"Please—"

"—I'm the one who needs pleasing, goddam it!"

She leaned back, spread herself, he tore off her panties, and rammed into her—over and over. She was just a thing to be used until he exploded with a roar.

Tears gushed from her eyes, just like his mother's that day long ago.

He pushed her off the countertop to the floor, grabbed her by the hair, and pulled her toward the bedroom.

He'd only just begun.

* * *

He took a long shower to wash away the blood that covered his chest. It felt good to put on the clean clothes Rosia had purchased.

Vlad did another search of Rosia's apartment for anything that might be of use to him. There wasn't much. He stuffed a few pieces of jewelry, a razor, and Rosia's money into a used grocery bag—he snatched up her car keys and quietly left the apartment.

At the doorway to the building, he looked up and down the street but didn't see anything suspicious. He moved to Rosia's Chrysler and, keeping low, crawled in on the passenger side. After a moment or two, he scooted over to the driver's seat, continued to keep his head down, started the car, and slowly drove away from the curb.

Chapter 45

Alex found it easy to follow Rosia when she left the health club.

He trailed her to a sketchy neighborhood; there were homeless people almost everywhere. Many were already setting up sleeping spaces behind garbage cans. He was surprised at the rundown neighborhood because it was only a short distance from where Rosia worked—which was in a decent part of town.

Alex parked and sat in his car, watching the building Rosia had disappeared into. After a while he wondered if perhaps his instincts were off. He began to question his actions—what was he doing here? Why had he followed her?

Mostly, it was because of the way the receptionist talked about the man in the photograph she'd shown him. He sensed a connection. Besides, she was his only lead at the moment.

He was deep into one of the *Mission Impossible* films, sneering at the definitely *impossible s*tunts, when he caught a flicker of movement out of the corner one eye. He snapped his head up just in time to see Rosia's black Chrysler coming slowly in his direction. When it was along side of him, he saw that it wasn't the receptionist driving.

It was Vlad Folo, who turned to stare at Alex for an instant.

He was angry with himself as he started the car and made a u-turn to follow his target.

Careless. Fucking careless. If he'd gone the other direction, I could have missed him all together. Then what? Another twenty years?

But that hadn't happened and he felt a jolt of pleasure pass through his belly. He'd been right to follow the receptionist and wait.

The Russian killer was now certain he'd found the damn kid.

Always in the eyes. They never change. And they were the same eyes that were in the finger-smeared picture he had of the boy with his parents.

He'd finally found Dimitri Antonev/Karl Pushkin/Vlad Folo. Up until now, he'd outsmarted Alex every step of the way.

Maybe he could finally complete his assignment and return home to Russia to his wife and children.

* * *

Vlad couldn't dare go back to his old apartment. And even if he was willing to risk it, he knew the twenty-five thousand he'd stashed was no longer waiting for him—the Pai Gow people would have taken it. Unfortunately, the money he'd taken from Rosia wouldn't last very long. He desperately need the fifty thousand from Tallent.

He could feel the walls closing in. He detested that trapped feeling. Why had he ignored the signs for so long?

When he was a little boy, his mother would talk about the *signs*. It was only after his parents were murdered that he truly understood what she meant.

The *signs* weren't really there—they were nothing you could see, or hear. You *felt* them in your gut, and they were usually right.

The *signs* had been screaming in his brain for a long time. He'd just ignored them.

I need to run! Get as far away from San Francisco as possible. Maybe get out of the U.S.

But—he needed the Tallent money.

With Gina Mazzio dead, he could take his money and run.

He asked himself again why he was struggling so hard to survive. Why fight it? In the end, did any of it really matter?

It was an old habit. He knew about habits better than most people.

* * *

Mort Tallent was sitting in his darkened living room, staring at the actors moving back and forth across the television screen.

The sound was on mute because he wasn't all that interested in what the characters had to say. Still, he tried to read their lips, a thing he'd picked up as a child when his parents didn't want him to hear them talking about him, and other things.

While he watched, he tried again to think about what he was going to do with the rest of his life. If he left medicine, how would he make a living? How would he spend his days?

Fool, you have plenty of money—if you didn't work another day, you'd still be raking in greenbacks from investments.

Those were the very words Annie would say when she tried to talk him into quitting medicine. He could hear her now: "Why do you keep doing something you hate?"

"It's all I know."

"Mort, you have enough money. Get out while you can."

"I'll go. But I need to wait until the end of the year."

It was the same promise he made over and over, year after year. Then one day she stopped asking ... and fell in love with another man.

Even now, after eighteen months, he still suffered, felt the pain of life without Annie.

She didn't have to die—you could have left her alone. Only you couldn't live with the idea of her being with another man, another man with his arms around her.

Tallent covered his eyes and tried to block out the mental image of Annie. Beautiful Annie.

For the hundredth time, he wished he'd never gone to the Time Out Health Club. Wished he'd never met Vlad. He was the one who planted the idea of killing Annie. Vlad pushed him over the edge.

Vlad the killer.

Killed Annie.

Killed Maria Benz and her mother.

Terrorized Lolly.

And now he's going to kill Gina Mazzio.

The doorbell rang. Tallent opened the front door and Vlad pushed past him.

"No lights?" Vlad flipped on a light switch and sprawled across the sofa.

"What's the matter with your face?" Tallent eased down into a chair across from Vlad. "And you look like a goddam bum dressed in those clothes. Don't you have any pride in yourself?"

"Oh, shut up! Your doorman liked the money I gave him to get my ass up here." He pointed to the TV screen. "Did I ask you why you're in the dark with a soundless television like some kind of creep?"

Tallent glared at him, wanted him out of his space.

"Besides," Vlad said, "I'm not the one asking for a favor. You sent me a note. And *you're* judging *me?*"

"Favor?" That struck Tallent as being funny for some unknown reason. He laughed and pointed to Vlad. "You call fifty grand a favor?"

"If you're going to be a smart ass, I'll leave, and let *you* settle this business yourself."

"Man, you really must run through the bucks. Otherwise, you wouldn't be here with your hand out, begging. You must have a very expensive habit of some kind." Tallent leaned back in his chair. "So, don't try to play games with me, Mr. Big Shot."

Vlad sat silently while they stared at each other. He blinked first.

"Okay, so who, exactly do you want me to do, that other nurse?"

"Yes. Gina Mazzio."

"I'll have it taken care of within the next few days. *But*, I need my money now."

"You think I keep fifty-thousand dollars sitting around in my apartment all the time, just in case? Forget it. That's what banks are for. All I have on hand is, maybe a couple thousand."

216

Vlad sprung up from the sofa and went down the bedroom wing hallway.

Tallent started after him.

Who the hell does he think he is walking in here and making himself at home?

But the moment passed. and Tallent sat back down in the living room.

What the fuck difference does it make?

* * *

Vlad walked on the plush, thick carpeting. He counted three bedrooms. One was fixed up as a den or study, the next one appeared to be a guest room, and the last one was obviously the master bedroom. He thought for a moment about taking it for himself, then decided he'd use the guest room for however long he was here.

But first he went into the study, where bookshelves lined two walls, a window took up another, and hanging on the fourth wall was an aqua surf board. He didn't know anything about surfing, couldn't understand why anyone would want to spend all that time in the water being worried about sharks. He could see, though, that this board wasn't for decoration—it had seen a lot of use.

On the same wall were many, many pictures of Tallent and the woman he'd killed for the doc some time back. The doctor looked much happier in all of the photos, many of which showed huge waves in the background.

So, this was the doctor's true love ... surfing.

He turned to the desk and methodically went from drawer to drawer. In the one with a large checkbook, there was also two thousand dollars in a neat, banded stack of new bills. He shoved it into his pocket next to the three thousand he'd taken from Rosia.

No matter how many times he turned everything upside down in the drawers, it was all the cash he could find. He wondered if there might also be a safe.

An anger-spiked iciness filled his chest.

He suddenly picked up a pointed letter opener, walked up to the surf board, and scratched his initials into its waxed perfection. When he finished, he smiled and threw the opener back onto the desk.

He went back to the master bedroom and looked through the drawers, lifting underwear and socks. In the closet, he chose a knitted sport's shirt and charcoal wool slacks.

He stripped out of the cheap, thrift store clothes and threw them across the quilted bedspread. He looked at himself in the mirror and although the shirt was much too roomy, the pants were the right length. He found a belt that he could tighten to fit his smaller waist size.

* * *

Tallent watched Vlad come strolling back into the living room, saw instantly that he was wearing his clothes.

"I see you helped yourself," Tallent said. "I have to admit you almost look human now."

"What would you know about that?" Vlad said and plopped down in a chair. He pulled a wad of cash out of his pocket, held it up for Tallent to see. "You were right, man. You had only two thousand in the house ... unless there's a safe hidden someplace."

"I hope you enjoyed yourself rummaging through my things—making yourself at home."

"It was quite informative." Vlad stuffed the money back into his pocket. "I'm gonna need to stay here for a day or two, Doc." He propped one foot up onto the coffee table.

Tallent started to object. "No—"

Vlad cut him off. "Once I've taken care of that nurse for you, I'll disappear—you'll never hear from me again."

Chapter 46

"I've got you, you bastard!" He couldn't stop shrieking with joy as he drove along a safe distance behind Vlad. Again and again, he pulled out a handkerchief to wipe away gushing tears of happiness.

Vlad Folo stopped at a high rise on the edge of Aquatic Park. Alex watched while Folo parked the Chrysler and entered the posh condominium building.

He circled around the block a few times before finding a parking spot where he could see the front of the building. He got out and walked over to the entryway, looked inside, spun on his heel, and went back to his car.

Not only was there a doorman, there was also a registration desk. Even if he could get past those two barriers, he had no idea where Folo had gone.

Alex sat in his car and swore an oath that he would not leave this spot until that miserable son-of-a-bitch came back.

For the first time in twenty years, Alex was happy.

He'd lived a monk's life in run-down hotels, existing on a pittance doled out by Leonid Solovief, his Russian boss. Now, the exile would finally come to an end. He would kill Vlad Folo, take a finger to prove he'd done in Dimitri Antonev/Karl Pushkin/Vlad Folo, and return to Russia.

He could hardly wait to tell his wife, but first he would call Leonid and inform him of the good news.

Alex took his precious sat-phone from the glove compartment and tried to compose himself. After several deep breaths, he tapped in the numbers that would connect him with Minsk.

"Da?"

"Misha? Is that you?"

"Da, who is this?"

219

"Alex ... Alexander Yurev."

Misha laughed so long he had difficulty catching his breath. Finally, he said, "Alex, we call you The Lost Russian. The last time Leonid spoke to you, you were still finishing our job of snuffing out the Antonevs."

Alex felt his blood turn to ice. "Where's Leonid?"

"Leonid is dead, my friend."

"What? When did this happen?"

"In the past summer." Again the laugh. "All over a piece of ass—imagine, at his age." Misha roared with laughter again. "Seventy-one years old and still acting like a young stud."

"Misha—"

"—the husband came home while Leonid was fucking the wife." Again, a roar of laughter. "Bang! Ha, ha! They were both dead. And of course, now so is the husband."

"I see," Alex said.

It was all so stupid." The phone suddenly went silent. "Why are you calling today, Alex?"

"I have found the Antonev boy. He will be dead within hours."

"Well, good. It only took you twenty years." Now the line was silent.

Alex could feel a jolt of heat in his belly "Who is the head man now?"

"Me." Misha's voice became a snarl. "I am the one you will talk to from now on."

"I plan on returning within two weeks. I miss my family."

"What family?"

Alex's heart was thrumming.

"You have no family, Alexander Yurev."

"But, my wife, Sophie, my sons ... my family."

Silence hung between them.

"Sophie is *my* wife now, Alex. She's still a beautiful woman. And your sons are now *my* sons. Do you understand? They are all mine!"

It couldn't be true.

"You're a lying piece of shit, Misha. You've always been a lying piece of shit!" Pain spiked through his chest. "Every week Sonya and me, we talk by Skype. She's said nothing to me."

"Why bother? We all knew you were never coming home again."

"But—"

"—now, my friend, you will always be known as 'The Lost Russian.'" The line went silent. "And you'll be The Dead Lost Russian if you ever set foot in Minsk again."

Alex felt faint as Misha's voice became a menacing growl.

"Do you understand me, Alexander Yurev? If you return to Minsk, you will The Dead Russian."

"I've worked hard for the organization. I've given up my family, my home. I followed the code—our code."

The line was dead.

Bette Golden Lamb & J. J. Lamb

Chapter 47

Gina and Harry were waiting for Christina Simon. The woman insisted on also meeting Gina before deciding whether to hack into Tallent's computer. Gina had never met a computer hacker and her curiosity was killing her. What kind of person did that sort of thing? What was she like?

Glasses of merlot in hand, and their feet up on the coffee table in the living room, they were talking about their dual wedding with Helen and Vinnie.

"Between the four of us, the number of people we're inviting is getting bigger and bigger." Harry nuzzled her neck. "At least you won't have to deal too much with my parents—they'll be lost in the crowd."

"Don't you think it's time we visited them? I really should meet them before we get married." Gina looked into his eyes. "How bad can they be when you're their son?"

"They're not bad. They're irritating and thoughtless. I don't want you to get hurt."

"I don't know—"

The phone rang.

"I hope it's not our hacker backing out." Gina struggle off the sofa and went across the room.

"Hello."

There was long pause.

"Hi, Gina."

"Lolly! Gina hit the speaker button so Harry could hear, too. "I've been leaving messages—you never answer. Are you all right?"

"I'm getting there," Lolly said. "It's been pretty difficult."

"Tell me what happened. Please?"

"I'm calling because I couldn't stop worrying about you." There was a long pause before she spoke again. "I meant what I

223

said before—stay away from Tallent. You hear me! Stay away from him!"

"I understand what you're saying, but I want to know what happened with you."

"Mort Tallent caught us on tape sneaking into his office."

"I know that," Gina said.

"What you don't know is that there's a maniac working for Tallent. The crazy man who killed Maria and her mother."

"He's the one who hurt you?"

"Gina, he didn't just hurt me. He interrogated me, he raped me, sliced me open, and tried to find out what we saw on Tallent's computer the night we snuck into his office."

"We didn't see *anything*. Did you tell him that?"

"Yes, yes, but he didn't believe me. He wanted your name and when I wouldn't give it to him, he cut me some more."

"Oh, Lolly. Have you been to a doctor?"

"As soon as I got here I went to a plastic surgeon." Gina heard a catch in her voice. "He said he'll do the best he can, but I'm going to be badly scarred, no matter what he does."

"I'm so sorry," Gina said.

"I'm the one who brought you into this mess, Gina. It's not your fault."

Is there anything I can do to help?"

"Stay safe!" Lolly paused. "Watch out for Tallent's hired murderer."

"I think he may have found me already. Someone has been following me. What does he look like?"

"Tall, very muscular—looks like he's on steroids," Lolly said. "And worst of all, he's a merciless cold killer. Just looking at him tells you that. This man would cut you into pieces and eat a chocolate bar at the same time."

"My God!"

"Stay clear of Tallent. You hear me, Gina? Stay clear of Mort Tallent no matter what else you do."

Lolly hung up without another word.

During the conversation, Harry had moved in close to Gina and heard most of the conversation on the speaker. "You know, doll, maybe we ought to back off on this whole hacking business. Let's stay out of Tallent's affairs. This is getting more bizarre by the minute."

"Tallent knows I'm involved." Gina wrapped her arms around his waist and looked into his eyes. "I think it may be too late to start doing the backstroke."

The door bell rang, Gina tapped the intercom button.

"Hi, who's there?"

"It's Christina."

"I'll buzz you in. We're upstairs."

"I'll go meet her and bring her up," Harry said.

Harry had told Gina that Christina was a woman who could take of herself. One glance when Harry ushered her in confirmed that.

Christina didn't waste any time. Her hand was extended to Gina right away as she stepped inside.

"Nice to meet you," Gina said, shaking her hand. "Let me take your wet jacket." She helped her out of a very damp pea coat.

"Would you like some coffee?" Harry said. "We just made a fresh pot."

"That would be great. Don't bother with any extra fixings. I like it black." She walked into the living room. "Man, I like that purple sofa."

"It was a steal." Harry held out a hand offering her a seat. "We got it at a garage sale. I won't tell you what we paid— you'll think we're thieves."

"Maybe you *are* a bunch of crooks since you're asking me to hack into a rich doctor's computer." Christina plopped down.

Gina came back with a cup of black coffee and handed it to Christina. She sat down in a chair opposite her. "The only thing we're stealing is information."

"You two really are babes in the woods," Christina said. "Information can be as valuable as cash in your pocket."

Her voice had hardened and Gina could see Harry was dead-on when he evaluated her the first time they met at Paul's. This woman wouldn't take crap from anyone. She would survive anywhere—even in the Bronx.

"So you think this doctor is a murderer?" She let out a cynical laugh. "Isn't that what they do legally, like all the time?"

"We think he hired someone to kill the woman who was taking care of his books," Harry said. "She got too close to the whole mess. Whatever she saw meant she had to be eliminated."

"You do this from your home?" Gina asked. "I mean, hacking. I know zilch about it."

"And let's keep it that way." Christina leaned back into the sofa and took several sips from her cooling coffee. "But, my group is not a gang of terrorists. We're the good guys. In fact, we've been uncovering some ISIS messages and tipping off Homeland Security. That's all I'm saying about that."

Gina smiled at Harry. "I think we found a winner."

Chapter 48

Christina Simon took a few days to think about the request to hack into Dr. Morton Tallent's computer files. What finally swayed her was that not only had she taken a liking to Gina and Harry, she trusted Paul Lucke. He was a stand up guy.

What struck Christina most about the couple was their unselfish motives—they weren't trying to rip off anyone, they were only trying to make things right. There weren't enough people in the world like that.

She hopped on a bus to her hacker buddy, Blitz. Whenever she went on what she called a 007 caper, she traveled by public transportation to keep as low a profile as possible. She also encrypted her emails and text messages.

Blitz lived near the San Francisco Zoo—claimed the only thing that kept him sane were his trips to see the animals. He really hated the idea of zoos—caging living beings—but he accepted that without them, most people would never understand how wonderful animals really are. His favorites were lions, but elephants were a close second.

Early on Christina had sexual fantasies about the tall, dark-haired Blitz. He was handsome in an offbeat kind of way, but she preferred men who were a little more testosterone-fired. The guy had no interest in women, or men, or much of anything else—not even money. After all, he was a trust fund baby who would never have to wonder where his next meal was coming from.

For Blitz, if it wasn't about computers, he didn't care.

Off the Muni, she walked along a couple of blocks that were lined mostly with two-story, pastel-colored homes common to the Sunset District. His house definitely fit the pattern—the residence of someone with a wife, 2.5 children, a dog, a cat, one car, and a regular 9-5 gig, probably even shopped at the co-op.

In Blitz' case, you'd be dead wrong.

Christina had phoned ahead because Blitz was pretty ugly when anyone just dropped by. She climbed the concrete steps to an enclosed entryway, gave the bell the required dot-dot-dot-dash signal, and Blitz answered the door within seconds.

He was wearing torn jeans and a t-shirt with a faded logo from an eight-year-old telecon. After a quick exchange of cheek kisses, they went straight to his workshop, which had been created by knocking out the wall between two bedrooms. There was barely room for the two of them to ease through the jungle of equipment, loaded shelving, and stacks of books and magazines.

There was one small loveseat near his main desk, half of it filled with paperback novels, all thrillers.

"Want something to drink, sweetheart?" he asked.

"No, I don't want a drink and you know how I hate that sweetheart shit." She walked over to the sofa and plopped down.

He gave her a wide smile. "Whadda ya gonna do? Ah loves it."

"And stop sounding like an idiot. A Harvard pee-aitch-dee doesn't talk that way."

"You're no fun, sweetheart." He sat opposite her on a rolling stool. "So what's the deal?"

"I was hoping you'd take time out and help this neat couple uncover a murderer."

"Murderer. Oh, oh, right. Okay, feed me the data."

he handed him a thumb drive. "It's in here, including his most recent password."

* * *

"You're sure this Gina and Harry combo is the real thing/" Blitz said after scanning everything on the drive. "I don't need any undercover snitches sending me off to the slammer."

"No, they're good people. They're only looking to out this creep of a doctor."

"Okay, let's get started."

Blitz pivoted around to face the arc of seven monitors. Just how many different computers they were linked to, Christina had no idea. Whatever the setup, lines of code scrolled across the screens in what seemed to be a never-ending stream of data.

"Okay, Leo baby, let's see what we can do here." Leo was his main computer, named after a beloved lion. A photo of the big cat sat atop almost every piece of equipment.

* * *

Gina and Harry offered to meet Christina at a semi-posh restaurant to go over her findings.

"Rather do it at your place," she said. "Never really know who the wait-staff are, or who's in the booth next to you. What say I bring over a little something and we can nosh while we talk?"

"Sounds nice, but the idea was that we would be treating you," Gina said.

"Six of one, half a dozen of the other."

"Around six, is that okay?"

It would have to be okay, but it meant changing plans they'd made with Helen and Vinnie to discuss more details for their joint wedding.

Gina picked up the phone.

"We'll have to cancel our dinner plans for tonight. A friend of Harry and Paul's is in town for just the day and they wanted to see her."

"No problem, sis. Tomorrow okay?"

"I think so," Gina said. "I'll let you know."

"So what's really going on, liar?"

"What do you mean? It's just what I told you." Gina could feel the heat crawling up the back of her neck. Telling a lie did that to her.

"Gina, you could probably get away with that phony excuse with almost anyone else, but not me. I know you. Something's up."

"Look, we'll talk tomorrow. Besides, why are you always so suspicious of me?"

Vinnie let out a loud laugh. "Are you kidding me?" And then he was gone.

"Sounds like Vinnie didn't buy your little white lie," Harry said while putting out some wine glasses. "Knew I should have called."

The bell rang, Gina opened the door.

"Oh, the parking around here is a bitch!" Christina stood in the doorway with a large take-out bag in her arms.

The aromas broadcast a bag filled with Chinese food. "Come in! Come in!" She took the food from Christina and carried it into the kitchen and sat in on the counter. Christina followed her.

"This is very sweet of you," Gina said.

"I agree," Harry said. "We would have been glad to make dinner."

"Two nurses?" Christina said. "Are you kidding? I knew it would be something like salad and fish or something healthy and boring. No way! Let's eat some real fun food." She looked around the small kitchen. "I assume you have chopsticks, right?"

* * *

They were sitting in the living room, Gina and Harry on the sofa, the hacker on a chair opposite them. Christina spread sheets of paper across the coffee table. She started explaining what Blitz and she found when they hacked into Tallent's computer.

"The man keeps two sets of books for his practice: One of them is for his consults and surgeries—they add up to close to a cool half-million a month. Most of the surgeries are listed as Cath Lab procedures. There's a number of triple bypasses, valve replacements, and blah, blah, blah."

"Blah, blah, blah is a new cardio surgical procedure?" Harry said with a laugh.

"I'm sure you'll be much more interested in some of the other stuff we found." Christina pointed to the spreadsheet on the table."

"He's just teasing you," Gina said.

Christina gave them the hint of a smile and continued. "The second set of books shows the same income/expense records as the first, plus entries for other financial activities, like double-billing Medicare and the insurance companies, plus blah, blah, blah. I'm not all that savvy with all this medical stuff, but it's sort of like ghost-chasing. It's probably what his accountant stumbled on."

"You mean the charges look phony?" Gina asked.

"Yep. Definitely cooking the books."

Christina scooted to the edge of her seat. "There was a separate password for an account named Vlad."

"Vlad?" Both Gina and Harry said at the same time.

"Now, that's really interesting. There are three fifty-thousand dollar entries in it, one from almost two years, another couple of weeks ago, and the third from only yesterday. Also, there's a twenty-five thousand dollar entry right after the second fifty." Christina's eyes were intense.

Gina did some mental calculations and said, "The dates sort of line up with the death of Tallent's wife, the deaths of Maria and her mother, and the twenty five is around time Lolly decided to pull up stakes and go back to New York. But the third fifty thousand entry?"

"Maybe he's hired Vlad to kill someone else that you don't know about," Christina said.

Gina and Harry looked at each other. He reached for her hand and squeezed it hard.

* * *

After Christina left, they looked at each other for a long time before walking back into the living room. They fell onto the sofa like twin puppets.

"Do you think Vlad's been hired to kill me? I mean, first it was Tallent's wife, then the bookkeeper and her mother, and now..."

"I know it looks bad," Harry said, but—"

"—Harry! He had me cornered in the locker room at Ridgewood. If you could have seen his face—it was a mask of pure malice. I could have some doubts that the man is a murderer if that hadn't happened."

Harry reached out and took her into his arms. "Let's think about it. God, I wish we could go to Mulzini about this."

"We can't do that." Gina squeezed him tighter. "He's scared about his own problems right now. We can't go to him."

"Calm down and think about it logically." Gina pulled away, looked at him, and nodded. "Why did he let Lolly live?" Harry said. "That doesn't make sense. I mean, he certainly wasn't bargain shopping at that stage of things."

"True. He could have thought it was way too soon for another murder, afraid he might interest the police."

"So Lolly just may have lucked out," Harry said.

"I wouldn't call what Lolly described as lucky. She ran away, maimed, and terrified."

"At least she's alive."

"All this for greed?" Gina asked. "You saw his financial run down."

"Maybe" Harry said, "but it looks as though once he took his wife out, it was like a domino effect."

"Yeah. And I'm the next domino set to fall!"

Chapter 49

Mulzini knew he was losing it. He'd been feeling crazy all day.

In all the years he'd lived and loved Marcia, he'd rarely made her cry. No credit to him. It was her. That woman really *got* him.

Pure luck that he'd found her.

Yet, twenty minutes ago she stormed out of the house, and as the door slammed shut, he heard, "You'd better get it together, Mulzini, or I'm never coming back—surgery or no surgery."

He pulled a chair up to the living room window and watched the rain come down in torrents. Marcia always said it was his dark side that drew him to the damp and rainy weather—made him feel better.

Not today. The only sunny side in my life just stomped out the door.

Dirk came and stood by Mulzini's chair—wrapped an arm around his shoulder.

"You know, Mulzini, I've been wanting to ask you a question for a long time. I just didn't know how you'd take it. Maybe this isn't the best time."

"Hey, kid. You can ask me anything—anytime, anywhere."

"Would you mind if I call you Dad instead of Mulzini?" Dirk smiled down at him.

It caught Mulzini off guard. He swallowed hard. "I was wondering if you'd ever come around to it." He stood, leaned over and buried his head in the kid's chest. Before he could stop himself, he started bawling.

"Hey, hey, if you don't want me to, don't worry about it. I know you already have kids and ... and ... really, I'll understand."

Mulzini stood and looked deep into Dirk's eyes. "Damn! I'd be honored, son. So would Marcia. You know how much we've come to love you."

"Thanks ... Dad!"

Mulzini smiled at him.

"Good! Now that we've got that out of the way ... and I already knew you'd say yes ... tell me, what the hell is going on?"

"Smart-ass kid." Mulzini walked across the room and plopped down on the sofa. Dirk followed and sat down beside him.

"It's this damn surgery. I don't mind admitting that I'm really scared."

Dirk took his hand. "Well, sure. Who wouldn't be?"

"But it's tomorrow; it's actually tomorrow."

"I know. But now isn't the time to push us away. You need Mom and me."

"Yeah, well, I don't like needing people—no matter how much I actually do. You get it?" Mulzini gave a humorless laugh.

Dirk nodded.

"I'm used to hoofing it alone, with my head up."

"It doesn't make you less of a person because you need people."

"And I believe that—for others. Not me." Mulzini smiled weakly and looked away.

"Dad, you're going to get through this with flying colors. Have I ever lied to you?"

"Well, yeah, I can think of a few occasions."

"Those don't count."

Then they were both laughing as Marcia came back through the front door.

She stared at Mulzini, defiance bouncing off every inch of her. "What's so damn funny, if I may ask?"

"I'm sorry, babe," he said. "Really sorry. And I need you to forgive me." He put an arm around Dirk's shoulder. "This one just asked if he could call me *Dad*." He turned to Dirk. "But no *Da-Da*. Got it?"

Marcia's scowl slowly morphed into a smile. "So you finally did it?"

Dirk nodded.

She leveled her eyes at Mulzini. "Just to let you know, he's been calling me *Mom* for the past month."

"How come I never picked up on that?" Mulzini slapped Dirk's thigh.

Marcia carefully removed her wet jacket, threw it on the floor, and jumped into his lap. "Because you're a lousy detective, Mulzini!"

* * *

Vinnie, Helen, Gina, and Harry stood outside the Mulzinis' front door, waiting for someone to respond to the doorbell.

Vinnie said, "Are you sure he won't mind our popping over like this on the night before surgery?"

"I don't care whether he minds or not," Gina said. "I know he's scared to death and I'm sure Marcia could use a little backup."

"And having us here is going to help distract him." Harry held up the huge box of pizza they'd brought with them.

"Need some help with that," Helen said. "Not that I'm offering—I'm just saying, the bottom is probably damn hot."

Dirk opened the door and Gina knew it was a good thing they'd come when he gave them a big smile.

"Hey, come on in. Dad's going to love this. Mom planned a nice intelligent dinner, but pizza? Dad's going to go wild."

Dirk stepped aside and they all marched into the living room. Mulzini and Marcia were holding hands and smiling.

Everyone started laughing at the look of surprise on Mulzini's face.

* * *

Gina and Mulzini found a corner in the living while the others were still eating around the kitchen table.

"You guys are something else." Mulzini held up a wedge of pizza "Thanks for this. I really do appreciate it."

"You know, every time I look at Dirk I remember that night after being dumped in the park and buried, he found me and really saved my life. I was so scared."

"You've always said it was cosmic." Mulzini had a toothpick trying to work out a piece of tomato caught in his eye tooth. "

Gina nodded. "He's a great kid."

Gina watched Mulzini's eyes fill with tears. She reached for his hand. "I know you're afraid. But look at it this way—you're having surgery in my department and I'll be in the thick of things, looking to save your ass."

"Does that mean you'll also have your hand inside my chest?

"Cool it! They are not opening your chest. They're going in to try to stop your atrial fib by buzzing some cells." Gina squeezed his hand. "Aren't you tired of that rapid heartbeat sending you to the ER?"

"Yeah, yeah. Of course I am. But that doesn't mean I want someone electrocuting me."

"They'll find the area in your heart where those bad cells are sending out the wrong signals. Then they'll shut them up."

"Now you're at least talking like a *mench* instead of some medical wizard."

"I love it when Italians speak Yiddish." She leaned over and looked into his eyes. "I'll be there for you, Mulzini. Just the way you've always been there for me."

"You're a good kid, Mazzio." He squeezed her hand. "But you're definitely a pain in the ass."

"I know. It's one of my more endearing qualities."

Chapter 50

Mulzini was on a gurney, on his way to the Cath Lab. He was wide awake, telling Gina over and over that he really didn't want to do this. He'd refused any pre-op meds, and kept insisting he wanted to get up and go home.

"You can't go home until you have your procedure." Gina pulled scissors from her jeans and waved them in front of his face. "Don't worry, Mulzini, I'll cut away all the bad parts, put them in a jar of formaldehyde."

"Hah! Very funny."

"Look, you're going to be fine."

"You're a liar." Mulzini tried to scoot off the gurney but the nurses held him down. "I know damn well that doctor is going to murder me."

* * *

Gina jerked up in bed, drenched in sweat. She could barely breathe.

Harry turned over, nudged her, and mumbled, "Go back to sleep, doll."

She was chilled when she lay back down. She scooted under the covers, cuddled up to Harry's back. She closed her eyes, and tried to relax.

A dream. Only a dream.

But she was afraid, worried it was a warning that Dr. Morton Tallent might end up killing Mulzini.

* * *

Tallent spent a restless night, turning from side-to-side, barely getting any sleep. Having Vlad in his house, in the next room, made him edgy. The guy was like a fuse, lit and ready to blow.

He finally turned on the light; the first thing he saw was his bedside picture of Annie. She'd had the softest eyes he'd ever seen. Even when she was angry there was always room in her heart for forgiveness.

He held the picture to his chest, tears blinded him.

I'm such a fool.

In the year before she left him, she did all the crying in bed at night, just as he was doing now. He would take her into his arms, try to soothe her. But even while he held her close, his head was filled with numbers: projected income, investment growth, the S&P, the Dow.

Money. Money.

At the crack of dawn, he crawled out of bed, padded down the hall, and went into his study. He looked around the room, his gaze moving from one item to another. He was searching for something, not knowing exactly what. Then he saw Vlad's name scratched across the surface of his surfboard.

That piece of shit knows he owns me. Owns my soul.

Tallent collapsed into his desk chair, stopped to look back and forth between the damaged board and another picture of Annie on his desk.

Everything he treasured had been stolen away while he was trapped in a snarl of numbers that he'd created.

It had all started when he heard of that dirty little secret where other doctors were overbilling Medicare with phantom charges. That first small step away from basic medical ethics had brought in huge profits, with no outlay of capital. He never once had to chase down Uncle Sam to pay its bills. The government coughed up the money like a super-efficient ATM.

It was so easy, it felt like magic.

Then he stepped away from the more risky surgeries and nailed every possible Cath Lab procedure, needed or not, and more and more money poured in.

More magic.

His net worth soared as cash turned into stocks and bonds, tax shelters, off-shore accounts. He'd become a Midas.

Blind, stupid, he hadn't seen it coming. Annie found someone else to love and appreciate her.

A judge had pointed a finger at him, warned it was now his responsibility to take care of his ex wife, pay for her upscale lifestyle with another man. He fumed, at first more angry at the loss of money than with the loss of his wife.

That's when Vlad-the-murderer stepped in.

Lolly Stentz was the lucky one. She'd seen the threat for what it was and ran. She escaped Vlad Folo.

Too late, Tallent understood it all.

Annie was gone. Maria Benke and her mother were gone, and soon Gina Mazzio would be gone—all because of him.

* * *

Tallent was reading the newspaper and finishing his third cup of coffee when Vlad oozed into the kitchen. He was like an apparition—one second Tallent was alone, the next Vlad was standing next to him.

"I have decided to leave sooner than I planned." Vlad sat down at the table and helped himself to an uninvited cup of coffee and a chocolate croissant.

Tallent didn't look up. "The sooner you leave, the better."

"Yes. I knew you'd feel that way. So, doctor, you and I are going to your bank so you can purchase a cashier's check—what you owe me to take care of the nurse."

Tallent lowered the newspaper. "I could write you a check right now, or don't you trust me?"

"I trust no one." Vlad stared him down. "Besides, why leave a paper trail? And you might cancel it once I walked out the door."

"I admire that," Tallent said, his voice sounding dead even to himself. "You do think things through."

Vlad blurted a humorless laugh. "Personal check or no personal check, remember, I could still make sure the police find what they need to send you away—for a long, long time."

"I never doubted it."

"Maybe you are getting smarter, because if you do something dumb, I *will* kill you."

* * *

Gina and Harry were paying for their morning coffee at the Ridgewood cafeteria when they heard Vinnie call to them from in back of the line. It was thirty minutes before they were due on the unit.

The two of them found a table for four, sat down, and waited for Helen and Vinnie to join them.

"You're worried, I can tell," Vinnie said to Gina.

"Of course she's worried." Harry squeezed Gina's hand. "Mulzini's not only a friend—the man's saved our tails too many times to count."

"I know. Mulzini's the best." Helen took a quick sip of her coffee and set her cup on the table. "I love the guy."

Gina knew Vinnie was studying her face. "Something's up. There's more to this than you're telling us, right?"

"Nothing, really, other than I'm worried." Gina put a spoon in her cup and stirred and stirred and stirred. "I just wish someone else was doing the surgery."

"None of us like Mort Tallent," Helen said. "How did Mulzini end up with him? Why didn't you steer him to Cantor or Brichett?"

"I tried. But Mulzini was in a hurry to get it over with and the other two guys didn't have any openings for moths. Besides, Mulzini's a grown man. We can't make those kinds of decisions for him."

Harry glared at Helen. "Why ask something like that now? Jeez."

"All right, let's not get all riled up," Vinnie said. "What time is the procedure scheduled?"

"He's second up. Probably about ten." Gina downed the rest of her coffee, looked at Harry. "I can't just sit here. I'm going to the unit."

Harry took hold of her hand. "I'll walk you up, doll."

She turned and waved goodbye, worried not only about Mulzini, but herself.

* * *

Outside the CCU, Gina and Harry held hands, turned to each other. People were coming on shift, walking around them. Gina barely noticed.

"Harry, what am I going to do? I can't risk having Tallent hurt Mulzini."

"Listen, doll, just keep your eyes open. That's the best way to protect Mulzini—and yourself. Besides, we don't really know that third payment has anything to do with you."

"That man I saw in the cafeteria and outside our apartment was following me. I know it."

"Maybe, but let's take care of one thing at a time." Harry leaned over and kissed her on the lips.

Gina took a deep breath and stood taller. "You're right! Mulzini and I have to get through the day, one minute at a time."

She gave Harry tentative smile, waved goodbye, and walked into the CCU.

Bette Golden Lamb & J. J. Lamb

Chapter 51

Stepping into the CCU, Gina hurried to the surgical area. She could see that all the ORs were running at full speed. Down the hall where the Cath Rooms were, the first patients were being taken from the holding cubicles for their procedures.

Gina flew to the central nursing station to check on the department schedule. Bob Cantor was in Lab One, Brichett in Lab Two. Both were doing ablations.

When Gina saw her assignment, she wanted to scream. Mulzini was up next and she was chalked in to assist Tallent.

She didn't want to even look at the man, but at least she would be right there to watch over her friend.

Gina hurried to the family waiting room. She was jumping out of her skin, but Dirk and Marcia were in the lounge trying to look calm. Gina knew how scared they really must be.

"Hi, you two." Gina reached out to hug Marcia, and then Dirk. "How are you guys holding up?"

"A walk in the park." Marcia looked as though someone had drained all her blood; her eyes were like huge saucers.

Dirk smiled, but when he turned away. Gina knew he was crying.

"Your sons aren't coming?" she asked Marcia.

"Mulzini wouldn't let me tell them." Marcia's arms were covered with goose bumps. "It's probably better this way. Less pressure on my guy."

"Well, I've got to get back. It won't be too long. In the meantime, they'll give him some meds to relax him."

"That'll be the day," Marcia said.

* * *

Harry was having trouble concentrating on the change of shift report. All he could think of was Gina, and how frightened she was.

He was frightened, too.

She'd been in a lot of dangerous situations—had a lot of near misses where she could have died. But no one had ever been paid to kill her. He couldn't wrap his mind around that.

The ICU census was light today, but even with fewer patients, the noise level was unnerving with the shrill alarms and buzzers constantly going off.

"Harry!"

"Yeah? What?" The team leader must have been asking him something—he was in a different zone, trying to come up with a plan to keep Gina safe.

"What's with you, Harry?" The team leader was looking at him, head tilted, brow furrowed. "Not like you to be off in the clouds. You're usually keyed and ready."

"Sorry. Personal problems."

"Is that Gina gal giving you a rough time?"

"You don't know the half of it."

* * *

Mulzini tried to focus on the nurses, running back and forth between him and another cardio patient.

He was handling it, but the man next to him was climbing the walls. He wouldn't shut up.

"What are you having done?" the guy asked.

"Ablation," Mulzini said.

"I know what that is. Mine's more serious."

"Look, man. I don't want to be rude, but you're making me more freakin' nervous than I already am." Mulzini gave him a nasty eye beating. "So if you could just zip it, I'd really appreciate it."

"You don't have to be such a douche-bag."

Mulzini half sat up. "You think I'm a douche bag now, you ain't seen nothing yet. So shut the fuck up!"

One of the nurses hurried into the room, syringe in hand. "All right, you two. Cool it!" She checked the ID bracelet of the big mouth and then added medicine into his IV. "You're next, Mr. Mulzini." She finished and hurried back out of the room.

Mulzini watched the guy's glare slowly disappear. After a while, he closed his eyes and was off to slumberland.

Jeez, it's about time! Thought he'd never shut up.

As promised, the same nurse returned with another syringe. "Your turn. Any questions before I give you this?"

He shook his head, saw Mazzio step up to his bedside. "Nora, can you give me a moment? Mulzini's a friend of mine."

"Sure. We have a little time." Nora turned and walked out.

Mulzini looked up at Mazzio, tried to come up with some kind of wisecrack. Nothing. Just plain too scared.

"This is going to be a breeze, Mulzini." She took his hand, squeezed it hard.

"Will you be around, Gina?"

Are you kidding me? You never call me anything but Mazzio."

"Gimme a break, will you? Are you going to be here?"

"I'll be in the same room. I may even talk to you now and then." She smiled at him. "But you won't remember any of it later." She bent over and kissed his cheek. "You'll be fine."

Nora was back in the room with her ever-ready syringe. Gina nodded to her and Nora injected the med into an IV port. "It won't be too much longer now, Stefano."

"Mulzini!" Gina and Mulzini said in unison.

Bette Golden Lamb & J. J. Lamb

Chapter 52

Alexander Yurev was slumped in his car, in a daze. He watched the sun rise, tried to envision what his future was going to be like.

What a fool I've been! Twenty hard years doing what I was told to do, thinking all along my Sonya was being faithful, raising our children, waiting for my return.

Idiot! Not my Sonya, Misha's Sonya. Misha, that disobedient, sex-crazed idiot!

Alex was painfully aware of what a loyal and naive grunt he'd been for the brotherhood. His life had dribbled away while he did penance for fucking up the Antonev assignment.

And now, Misha had stolen his woman and children while he wasted away in America.

He hadn't slept during the night, cramped up in the car. All he could think about was Misha and how he would return to Russia and kill him.

But first, he would destroy this Vlad Folo, this Antonev/Pushkin kid who had gotten away from him time after time. And there would be no doubt when he cut off Folo's finger as proof that he had completed his assignment. Folo was as responsible for his destroyed life as was Misha. Together, they had held him prisoner.

After talking to Misha, he'd forced himself to stay with the car and keep watch for Folo. The bastard would not get away this time.

He ordered a pizza and drinks to be delivered to his car and when the streets were deserted, he relieved himself in the bushes like a street dog.

Yes, that's what he had become: an abandoned, killing animal.

* * *

Vlad watched the doctor as he left the apartment. Yes, this man, this doctor with the slumped shoulders, had given up all hope.

He knew Tallent would pay all of Vlad's money demands, not only now, but through the coming years—whatever it took to save his miserable ass.

Vlad didn't like the doctor, never had. He had to hold back a constant urge to kill the coward, put him out of his misery. But Vlad needed money more than the satisfaction of taking the doctor's life. If he was to start over again, with a new identity and a new home, he would need Tallent's money.

And so he would kill the nurse for him.

He had studied the Mazzio nurse, watched her with her man in the hospital cafeteria, and watched her outside her apartment building. The woman had a fire in her belly, she would fight hard for her life.

He'd had women like her before. But they all gave in, sooner or later.

Breaking someone's spirit wasn't all that difficult. All he had to do was convince them that he definitely would kill them. Easy. No problem.

Vlad smiled, content with himself. Yes, he *was* a good killer.

He went out to Rosia's car, but didn't get in immediately. Something was off—something he couldn't quite identify. He looked around, along the sidewalks, up and down the street; inspected the windows of the tall, high-rent apartment buildings all around him.

The signs were there again. A chill crawled up and down his back. Who? How? From where?

Jumpy.

He checked his watch.

It was late morning. He drove to a little neighborhood cafe he knew. He would eat, take a nap in the car, and be ready.

* * *

Alex walked into the little café where Vlad was eating, tried not to attract the man's attention. He slowly, quietly found a seat two booths away, toward the rear of the cafe, and to Vlad's back.

He edged onto the vinyl-covered seat and waited for the shapely waitress, in a bright yellow uniform, to come to him after taking Vlad's order.

"Coffee?"

"Yes, that would be good. I would also like some bacon and eggs with rye toast."

"Like I told the man at the other table ... ten minutes more and you would have missed breakfast." The waitress smiled at him, showing the whitest teeth he'd ever seen. "Coming right up."

When he looked up, Vlad had turned around and was looking directly at him. Alex nodded, got up, and went to the men's restroom.

Inside, he stared at his image and could see he was a mess. Not as terrible as he felt, but his plain blue tie was askew and his shirt was grubby. It didn't matter much. His rain coat did a good job of covering most of his wrinkled clothing.

He bent over and washed his face with cold water, then pulled a comb from his pocket and ran it through his hair. After fixing his tie and brushing off his raincoat, he didn't look quite as grubby as before.

* * *

Vlad didn't like the looks of the man who came into the café right after him. And when he heard him give his breakfast order to the waitress, he thought he heard an accent, a Russian accent. But the man was soft-spoken and too far away for Vlad to be certain.

He watched the man get up and go to the restroom. There was something about him, something other than his near-bum appearance. Vlad was tempted to leave, then tried to calm himself—he'd been far too jumpy the last few days, and for no real reason that he could identify. Besides, he was here and he was hungry. If this man was a danger, Vlad was more than ready to handle it.

When the man returned, Vlad could see that he'd kind of pulled himself together. He wondered if he was perhaps some kind of traveling salesman. Then he noticed that the man walked with a slight limp. Vlad relaxed. The brotherhood wouldn't send someone to take him out who wasn't in the best shape possible.

He smiled at the young waitress when she brought his breakfast of pancakes and sausage. He dug into the food and forgot about the man a couple of booths behind him.

Chapter 53

Tallent stood in front of the bulletin board in the Nurses' Station. He studied the surgery lineup, couldn't believe that Gina Mazzio was scheduled to scrub in with him for the policeman's cardio cath.

He took off for the locker room—needed some space to think. The place was empty—everybody was out on the unit floor, where he should be.

He collapsed on the narrow wooden bench between two rows of ceiling-to-floor metal lockers. He rested his elbows on his knees, cupped his chin in both hands. His mind did cartwheels as he took in deep breaths.

Pull yourself together.

He had to focus on the procedure he would be doing in a few minutes. He needed to get his ass in gear and start thinking about Stefano Mulzini and his ablation. Instead, his thoughts bounced between Mazzio, Vlad, and Annie.

Stop it!

He reached in one pocket, then in another for the oversized shoe coverings and his cap. He had to get to the scrub room, get ready for the procedure.

His mind flashed to Stinson Beach, where he and Annie practically lived—until his parents revoked his trust fund.

There was no more money. Do it their way—or else!

Another mind jump and he remembered that the first official day of the Mavericks surfing competition would be coming up soon. He could picture the famous rock-studded surf spot twenty miles south of Francisco. He'd been good back then, really good. He and his surfboard rode the waves together, like a superhero—Batman and his Bat mobile.

He smiled, remembering the fifty-foot wave that tossed him into the sea, and his near-suffocation when another wave hit and held him under. He'd barely escaped. But he never told Annie about it. Nothing was ever going to stop him from surfing.

Nothing other than a revoked trust fund.

He still resented the power his parents had held over him. They'd put him in a box with no openings. His father got him reinstated to the Stanford School of Medicine, rented a small house in Palo Alto for him and Annie, and set up no-cash-back credit card accounts to cover living expenses. But no cash.

He still found an hour here and there to surf, but having to be extra careful not to break his board took a lot of the pleasure out of it.

Fool!

* * *

Bob Cantor finished his procedure and left the Cath Lab, shucking his gloves and loosening his gown. He was dripping with sweat.

His patient was okay following a tricky cardiac angioplasty that had gone much longer than anticipated because the man had required two stents instead of one to open up clogged arteries,

But now his patient was in recovery and doing fine. As soon as Cantor was convinced he was stable, he would send him on over to CCU as an in-patient, where he would spend the night under close observation. If all continued to go well, Cantor would discharge him, probably tomorrow.

With a couple of hours on his hands until his next case, Cantor decided to drop in to see his in-house patients.

I must be getting old. I'm really beat.

Not only that, both he and Jon Brichett had been working overtime to take on many of Tallent's patient referrals. His books were closed—no more new patients.

It was a relief in many ways. It had become obvious that Tallent had no love for practicing medicine. What he did love was raking in money.

Cantor wondered if Tallent would really just take some time off or end up leaving their practice all together. Trying to talk to the man privately had become useless. He'd dodged meeting after meeting with him and Burchett.

He and Tallent had been friends at one time—maybe not close, buddy-buddy great friends, but they were always respectful of each other. Until recently. Now they barely spoke, even when riding in the same elevator.

Cantor was on the way to the locker room to change into fresh scrubs when Gina Mazzio grabbed his arm.

"Bob, I need your help."

Gina's face was flushed and she was breathing like a race horse after a run. She was barely able to talk.

"Hey," he said, "what's the matter?"

"My friend Mulzini is having a cath shortly."

"Okay. What's the problem?"

"He signed up with Mort Tallent. Your waiting list was too long and Mulzini is a full-blown Type A. He wouldn't listen to anybody about a possible delay one once his mind was made up to do the procedure."

"So?" Cantor said, puzzled.

"There's something wrong with Mort. I don't trust him anymore."

Somehow, Gina had pushed the wrong button—whether it was because he was unhappy with Tallent himself, or because he was just plain tired.

"What is it with you, Gina? Aren't we running our practice to suit you? I mean, we brought Lolly Stentz into our practice because you recommended her. Didn't you vouch that she was top-notch?"

"Yes, I did. She's a great nurse."

"Okay, so where is she? And if she's so great, why did she up and walk out on us without word of warning? Our offices were left high and dry, critically short-staffed." He tossed his gown into a nearby laundry container.

"It was an emergency. She *had* to leave."

"I've known you a long time, Gina. Your word usually carries a lot of weight with me, but I'm beginning to wonder about your judgment lately. And now, you're making unwarranted accusations about Mort's competence. Who the hell do you think you are?"

Her arm dropped away from his and he watched her face morph from surprise to anger.

"I really don't give a damn what you think of me, Bob. But I do know you care about your patients. All I'm asking is for you to please stick around until Mulzini is in recovery. Please!"

He watched her, head held high, flip around and head for the Cath Lab scrub area.

Chapter 54

Mulzini was moving, floating. Instead of trying to listen to the voices around him, he surrendered to the lulling motion. He knew he was giggling because it reminded him of being a kid in a flimsy cardboard box, flying down a hill. There was still an echo of joyous laughter in his head from long, long ago.

He opened his eyes and stared into the overhead lights whizzing by.

He was out of the cardboard box now and thinking about his telescope, tucked away at home in the storage closet. It was there with all kinds of other things that had been put aside as not being important. He remembered carrying the telescope outside and setting it up on the sidewalk so he could study every quadrant of the night sky—always ending up indulging in his main fascination, the moon.

Whenever he would share that memory with Marcia, she would laugh and call him a "Moonie," even though she knew that any mention of that defunct cult always got his hackles up. He had a hunch she did it to get a rise out of him—which it always did.

Funny lady.

He heard someone say, "Mr. Mulzini, we're positioning you under the equipment now."

"'S Mulzini ... jus' Mulzini

"Hey, Just Mulzini. It's me. I'm here too."

"'Zat you, Mazzzzz...i...o?"

"Yeah. Think I'd lose an opportunity to finally have you in my power?"

He started to drift off. "Poor, Mazzio ... my trouble-shooter ... trouble-maker ... trouble ... trouble ... toil 'n trouble..."

* * *

Gina watched Mort Tallent in the other room, scrubbing for the procedure. She usually liked the glass partition that allowed her to see outside the Cath Lab, it kept her from feeling claustrophobic. Today, even with Tallent's face mostly covered with a mask, she could still see his piercing eyes shooting pure malice at her.

Tallent knows Mulzini's my friend. Would he dare to take his anger at me out on him?

What an idiot she was. Why hadn't she been more open with Mulzini—insisted he change doctors?

And why hadn't Bob Cantor listened? Why was he so angry at her? Most of all, why wasn't he here to save her friend?

All Gina could think of was helplessly watching Mulzini die on that table because of her and Lolly. And they hadn't then even found anything.

Now, she and Harry knew that everyone of those fifty-thousand dollar payments were to someone named Vlad. Each payment corresponded to when Tallent's wife was murdered, when Maria Benke and her mother were murdered. The twenty-five thousand was the same time Lolly ran away. And the final fifty? Gina was certain it had her name on it.

Not going to happen! Tallent and this Vlad guy are going down.

When she finished the shift, she was going straight to Inspector Pepper Yee—a Mulzini cohort. There hadn't been a lot of trust between Yee and Gina, but the cop would do her job. If they were suspicious of Tallent in the past, it shouldn't take much to arouse their attention again.

If only Mulzini hadn't been sick—he would have believed her right away. He would have at least tried to help.

Gina finished with last minute details in setting up the instruments and equipment that Tallent would need. She decided that after the ablation, Tallent would kill Mulzini, if that's what he planned. Or it could happen like it did with Kat Parker—the result of his carelessness.

The team leader, Gwen, was the circulating nurse today. Right now she was checking Mulzini's vitals and administering more meds.

"How are you feeling," Gwen ask Mulzini.

"I keep drifting off into nowhere land. This is the best rest I've had in a long time."

"That's good. Just keep in mind, we're going to keep bugging you. This *is* a hospital ... we can't let you get too much rest."

Gina's stomach was a cauldron and her knees almost failed her when Tallent walked into the procedure area.

She handed him a sterile towel to dry his hands, then helped him into his gown and gloves. He seemed to lose his way for a moment, adjusted, nodded at Gina, looked at the equipment on the table, then stood there staring off into space.

The nurses and technicians were all waiting for the procedure to begin, but Tallent kept his gloved hands folded across his chest.

"Doctor?" Gina prompted.

He slowly turned, looked directly into her eyes. She could see he really wasn't in this room ... he was someplace else that she couldn't even imagine.

Everyone seemed caught in a time-lapse, looking at one another, each probably wondering what to do next.

Then she saw Bob Cantor through the glass partition in the scrub area, making preparations to step in. When he came in, he stepped up close to Tallent and said, "I'll get this one, Mort."

* * *

Tallent could swear he heard the sound of the ocean as he slowly returned to the locker room.

No, he wasn't imagining it. The crashing waves kept roaring in his head.

In the hospital garage, he got into his Mercedes, and sat very still for a long, long time.

Chapter 55

Gina was both exhausted and exhilarated when Mulzini's procedure was finished—everything had gone smoothly. He was in great shape, headed for post-op.

Working with Cantor had been wonderful. They were a great team.

"So I'm a jerk, right?" Cantor said as he started out the door of the Cath Lab.

"Can't argue with that." Gina was gathering the instruments, getting them ready to be cleaned. She was determined to remain calm even though she was still annoyed by the way he'd treated her. It didn't work.

"Why all the hostility? I thought you and I got along pretty good. You always seem to trust my judgment ... until this morning."

"That's not fair, Gina. I came, didn't I?"

"I guess that's *something*."

"You need to understand, things are unsettled around here. I don't know whether you know it or not, but Mort's taking a leave of absence from his practice. Frankly, I don't think he'll return to medicine."

"After this morning, I think we can agree that's a good thing."

"Maybe so, but Jon and I are having to take up the slack. We're not only overworked, we're kind of pissed at the guy."

"You're better off without him, Bob. This morning doesn't even cover it all."

"Maybe, but I didn't get into medicine to work myself to death."

"Why does anyone get into medicine?" Gina said. "It's because we want to help people."

259

"That's an idealistic fantasy that most of us start out with. We all look for that rosy future, but it doesn't take long before reality smacks us in the eye. If we could only just treat patients." He let out a big sigh. "There's so damn much paperwork—insurance forms, Medicare forms, federal forms, state forms; it goes on and on and on. The partnership eases that burden somewhat, but the worst thing for me personally is watching people die because they can't afford expensive, over-priced meds." He turned away. "I'm tired of it all."

"All I know, is that this morning you saved a life."

* * *

At the end of the shift, Gina went to check on Mulzini. Marcia and Dirk were already there, sitting in chairs next to the bed, talking softly. When she looked at the man of the hour, he was sound asleep, snoring softly.

"Look at him," Marcia said. "He hasn't slept like that for weeks. Now that it's over, he'll probably have to sleep most of every day for a week just to catch up."

"Yeah, he hasn't been himself much lately," Dirk said. "It's been tough, especially on Mom."

Hearing Dirk say "Mom" made Gina smile. The kid had really found a family that loved him. She still remembered him alone, lost, sleeping in the park, and fighting off sexual predators to survive.

"Everyone is pleased with how it went," Gina said.

"Thanks for all your help," Marcia said. "I'm really grateful."

Gina bent over and gave her a hug. "Well, I gotta go. Tell him I love him, mean old grump that he is, and that I'll see him tomorrow."

Walking down the corridor, Gina pulled out her phone and tapped in Harry's number.

"Hi, babe," he said. "Just finishing up my notes. Where are you?"

"Just leaving CCU. Dropped in to see Mulzini."

"Sure he had plenty to say. How is he?"

"Done in and asleep."

"Wait for me," he said. "I'll meet you at the elevator."

"I'm beat ... going to head on down; meet you at the car instead."

"Gina, wait for me! Please!"

"Harry! You're being a bear." She was too happy to stand still doing nothing. "I'll meet you down stairs."

When the elevator arrived, four other people were inside. Stepping out into the garage, everyone turned left except her. She turned the other way, right into the arms of a man who smothered her face into his chest.

She punched at him, tried to yank free, but his steel grip locked around her, pinning her arms to her sides. He slammed her hard in the neck.

Gina dropped and spun into nothingness.

* * *

Harry ran like a mad man, ran to the locker room, grabbed his coat, and jumped into an open elevator. He pounded on the garage button; two other passengers stared at him and stepped back to the rear of the car.

"It's not gonna go any faster, not matter how many times you pound that button,"

one of them said.

Harry nodded and punched the button again.

When the elevator door opened at garage level, he sprinted to where Gina had parked the Fiat that morning.

It was there, but Gina was nowhere in sight.

He pulled out his cell and called her.

This wasn't right, not after she'd said she would meet him at the car. And if she'd been delayed by someone or something, she would have let him know.

He tried to call her again, same results. If it hadn't been for that hired killer stalking her, he would have waited a while longer. Instead, he speed-dialed the SFPD.

"This is Sgt Jaspers. How may I help you?"

"My name is Harry Lucke. I need to speak to Inspector Pepper Yee."

"Regarding?"

"Please tell her it's about Gina Mazzio."

Harry was jumping out of his skin waiting for Yee to pick up.

"This is Inspector Yee."

"Do you remember me, Inspector? Harry Lucke?"

"Who could forget you, or that dingbat girlfriend of yours? Gina Mazzio, right?"

"Please, please listen! I think Gina's been snatched from the garage at Ridgewood Hospital. I really need your help."

"How long has she been missing?"

"It just happened." Harry could hardly speak, all his words spilled out on each other.

"I wouldn't call that missing, Harry." Her words were short and sarcastic. "If she's still missing in the morning, we'll talk."

"But, Inspector."

Inspector Pepper Yee had hung up.

Chapter 56

Harry ran back to the elevator, punched the #5 button, pulled out his cell, and once more tried to call Gina. The call went immediately to her mailbox.

"Damn it!"

Stepping out of the elevator, he hurried to Mulzini's room. The Inspector was awake, talking quietly with his wife and son.

"Hi, Harry! I hear I just missed Gina. Best sleep I've had in months."

Harry didn't know what to do. Mulzini needed to left alone, but the inspector was the only one he knew who would understand the situation. His heart was banging against his chest; his fear had left him weak and almost useless.

"Yeah." He couldn't say any more than that.

"Are you all right?" Marcia said.

Dirk stood, half-led Harry to his chair.

"What's up, Harry?" Mulzini pushed up onto his elbows.

"I think Gina's been kidnapped." He bent over and covered his eyes.

Harry could hear the Inspector take a couple of fast breaths. "Are you sure?"

"Would bet on it. I spoke to her right after she got off shift. We were supposed to meet in the garage. I couldn't have been more than a couple of minutes behind her. When I got there, she wasn't there and she doesn't answer her phone."

"Whose feathers did she ruffle this time?" Mulzini's face had paled. Marcia reached for her husband's hand.

"Do we have to do this right now, Harry?" Marcia said. "He's just out of recovery."

Mulzini shook his head. "Let him talk, Marcia."

"Short version," Harry said. "The doctor who was supposed to do your surgery, Tallent, is involved in some serious illegal business practices. He may also be involved in murder. Gina's certain he's paid someone to kill her." Harry paused. "Don't ask me how we know all this because I can't tell you, at least not right now."

"What do you mean 'the doc who was supposed' to do my surgery?"

"Tallent sort of spaced out on them and Gina got Bob Cantor to do your surgery."

"Well, that explains why that doctor was in here checking on me. He said Dr. Tallent was unavailable."

"Yeah," Harry said. "That's certainly the truth."

"Have you reported all of this to the police?" Marcia said. She poured some water into a cup and passed it the inspector.

"Why don't I answer that?" Mulzini said. "You tried, right?"

Harry nodded.

"But they won't look into a missing person incident for twenty-four hours."

"I'm really lost," Harry said. "And frightened. Don't know what to do to get someone out there right now." He looked at Mulzini, willing him to come up with a plan. "Gina could be dead by morning." Tears slithered down across his cheeks.

"Cool it, Harry. Gina's a tough cookie." Mulzini eased back down until he was flat in the bed again. "Who'd you talk to at the station?"

"Pepper Yee. Gina has dealt with her in the past. Sounds like she has a real grudge against Gina."

"I wouldn't go that far," Mulzini said. "But she sure as hell doesn't like her. Thinks she interfered in one of her cases. Knowing Gina, that could be true enough." He motioned for Harry to stand by, then picked up the bedside phone and put in a call.

"Hi, Pepper?"

264

"No! That you, Mulzini?" She laughed into the phone. "There's a rumor you went under the knife this morning. Is that true?"

"Yeah. Why, did you think I died or something? If so, you'd better think twice. Can't get rid of me that easily. I'll be back soon enough to get you off your duff."

"Seriously, how are you, old man?"

"Smug little thing, aren't you?"

"What can I do for you, as if I didn't know," she said.

"What do you mean?"

"I mean, whenever anything happens to that nut case Mazzio, you hop to it. I swear, you have a thing for nurses."

Mulzini's voice almost turned into a growl. "If you were smart, you would too. They damn well have saved a lot of cops. When are you gonna get that into your thick little skull?"

"All right already," she said, still cheeky, but the chip on her shoulder seemed to be slipping.

"Harry, Mazzio's fiancé—"

"—I know who the dude is."

"Bottom line, she's been taken."

"Mulzini, I'm not going to get into this with you. You may jump at the drop of a raindrop about anything that has to do with that broad, but I do it by the book—or at least as close as possible. I'm not doing anything, at least until morning. And even that's not twenty-four hours."

"You listen to me, hot shot: You get this rolling now or I'll make it my life's goal to make sure you end up out on patrol again. And I don't mean riding around in a squad car. You got that, Pepper?"

Mulzini disconnected, put his cell back on the bed stand. Harry could see that talking to Inspector Yee had pretty much done him in. Marcia was giving him the get-outta-here eye.

"I'm going to the patient waiting room and see if I can pull myself together. If I go home, I'll be tempted to call Vinnie and tell him what's going down. That would really be a bad thing for everyone—but especially him."

"Look, Harry, I guarantee Pepper will get on it." He turned on his side, reached for Harry's hand. "We'll get Gina back."

Chapter 57

Gina was dazed. A hot dagger stabbed into her neck and her head was pounding. When she opened her eyes, there was only a wall of impenetrable black.

The loud jarring rhythm of tires thumping on the road made her dizzy. All she could remember was walking out of the elevator into the employee garage.

She felt around—she was in a tight space, knew she'd been stuffed into the trunk of a car.

Oh, my God!

A car trunk!

Terror squeezed her belly.

Someone has grabbed her.

Her breath burst in explosive gasps and her chest caved with claustrophobia. A rasp of air warned she was starving for oxygen—she needed to shut down a sudden vision of being thrown in a coffin—alive.

She groped for her purse—her fingers flew over and around all the things she'd shoved inside. Her Swiss Army knife was there. She pulled it out and buried it in her scrub's pant pocket.

Her cell phone was gone but her small halogen flashlight was there. She used the beam to cut through the darkness.

Yes, she'd been stuffed into a trunk and she could barely move. Everything was closing in around her. She banged the top and screamed.

"Help! Help!"

She had nothing other than her jack knife to use as a tool..

The car slowed; it was being parked. Then, without any warning, the trunk flew up and she was staring into the eyes of the man who had been following her.

It was dusk, but she could see he was looking at her like a useless piece of nothing. He held a stiletto up so she could see it.

"One way or another, you are coming with me. If you scream, do anything to try to attract attention, I will stab you through your eye—or through your heart—or through your throat." He pushed his face closer to hers. "Do you understand?"

She nodded.

He grabbed her hair, digging his fingers into her scalp, and lifted her head above the edge of trunk. "Take a good look around you. In this neighborhood, you could shriek your head off and no one would open a door, or raise a window shade. If I kill you, no one will give a shit. Got it?"

She nodded again.

"You are going to die one way or another. How long you live is up to you."

* * *

Inspector Pepper Yee stared at the telephone—hadn't stopped staring at it since talking to Mulzini.

Damn that man! Even from a hospital bed he has me feeling guilty about that weirdo nurse.

Yee had seen enough of that woman a few years back. More than enough.

She swung her legs up, planted her heels on the edge of the desk. In another couple of hours she was going home, get ready for a date with a guy she really wanted to spend time with. Tall, blond, buff like she couldn't believe. He was the first man she'd had any real interest in since she and her husband divorced two years ago.

Now this.

She could let this whole Mazzio business wait until morning, just like she'd said to Harry Lucke—right now it was really too early to jump in, other than start the paper work.

But there was Mulzini. He'd asked her to run with it ... now. She owed him—owed more payback than to any other cop on the force.

Yee picked up a pen sitting idle on her desk and pushed the button at the top, snapping it open and closed—again, again. and again.

"Hey, Yee, knock it off before I hammer your head," yelled one of the guys further down the row of desk. "I'm trying to think."

"Nothing's gonna help you pull that off." She laughed, let her feet slide off the desk to the floor again. She pulled out her cell and tapped it.

"Hi, Jason. This is Pepper."

"Couldn't wait to see me, huh?"

"True enough, but we're going to have to take a rain check." She once more clicked the pen she'd refused to let go of.

"Not again!"

"I know. Nothing I can do about it. I'm off in a couple of days for forty-eight hours. How does that work for you?"

"Call me when you're finished today—no matter what time it is. We'll talk about it then."

She killed the connection, pulled up her emergency numbers on the computer, and picked up a land line, punched in the numbers and waited.

"Ridgewood Security, Tom speaking."

"Tom, this is Inspector Pepper Yee of the SFPD. I need to check your security tapes for the elevator that goes to the employee parking area."

"For twenty-four hours?"

Pepper could picture him cringing. "No, Just the past three hours."

"Okay, when do you want them?"

"I'm on my way now."

Chapter 58

Mort Tallent stood in his spacious living room, staring out the panoramic window at San Francisco Bay.

He was confused ... so many unanswered questions.

My life has been nothing but unanswered questions.

One thing was certain: this morning he stepped away from the practice of medicine ... forever.

By now, word of his actions, or inaction, during surgery would be spreading throughout the hospital, not stopping until it reached administration.

He couldn't return to that life now, even if he wanted to.

And he didn't want to.

He had enough money put away to do most anything, most anywhere.

That possibility had been on the table for a long time. He could have done it with Annie that time when she asked him to do it. They could have run away, done anything he wanted to do. Anything *they* wanted to do.

Together.

Too late for that, Tallent.

Way too late.

* * *

It had taken time for Mort Tallent to straighten up and clean his apartment, especially the kitchen and the room that Vlad had taken over.

Afterward, he took a shower to get the feeling of Vlad's slime cleansed from his body. He had to scrub long and hard before he was satisfied. By then, his skin was raw in places.

He threw a few things together, tied the marred surfboard to a luggage rack on the roof of the Mercedes, and drove north along the coast on Highway One.

At Point Reyes, he spent some time just taking in Tomales Bay before stopping at a local cafe for an oyster sandwich. Only after taking the last bite did it come to him that had to be the best sandwich he'd had in a long, long time.

It had been raining on and off since he left the city, the kind of day they'd been having around the Bay Area for the past month or so. It was wonderful.

He continued to drive west until he could see the Pacific Ocean. The storm-tossed water looked powerful, restless, and beautiful.

He called Vlad's cell, left a message: "Keep the money. Forget about Gina Mazzio."

After that, he felt calm, at peace with himself.

He turned the car around and headed back south through Marin County, across the Golden Gate Bridge, through San Francisco, and down the Peninsula to Half Moon Bay. The whole time the rain came down in torrents, several times so forceful the windshield wipers couldn't keep up and he had to pull off to the side of the road. Driving again, everything was drenched, cleansed. It was like the whole world was ready to start over. New beginnings for everything.

Except for him.

* * *

It was getting very late in the afternoon by the time Tallent changed into his wetsuit and carried his surfboard to a spot north of Half-Moon Bay. He looked at Vlad's name scratched on the board's polished surface. Vlad had taken over his life, owned him.

"No more!" Tallent screamed into the wind.

A light rain was still coming down, the tail end of the most recent passing storm. He watched the Maverick swells turn into waves that seemed to climb up into the sky before crashing back down and extending out to the shore.

He could picture Annie, smiling at him as if he were the only man in the world. He'd liked that feeling she gave him.

What he didn't like was that he'd never let her know that she was the only woman in world for him.

"Time to go!" he announced to the wind.

He hurried to the water, waded in, stretched out on the board, and started paddling. Soon, that's all there was: paddling, breathing, laughing, then again and again.

He caught the one big wave he was looking for, came up on the board, rode the crest, and when it started to curl under, he twisted around into the tunnel, and for one long moment he was in the eye of the universe. Then he drove into the monstrous wave, flipped up, over, and down, surrendering to his destiny.

Chapter 59

Vlad grabbed the nurse by the arm and back of her neck, lifted her out of the trunk, and stood her on the sidewalk. She was obviously scared, but there was also a simmering defiance in her eyes that made him cautious..

He started herding her toward the entrance to Rosia's apartment building. He felt a riffle of air around him, looked, saw nothing or no one. He shivered. Perhaps it was one of those feelings that, as his mother used to say, occurred when someone walked across your mother's grave.

Stupid superstition. Besides, her bones are mixed in there with all the other Potter's Field nobodies.

He shook off the chill that rode his back.

What difference did it make anyway?

The Mazzio woman was looking around the street; he was taking too much time, needed to get her inside.

"Where are you taking me?"

"Just go where I point you!" He poked the stiletto into the cheek of her ass.

They went through the entrance, where a homeless guy was splayed out on the dirty, broken tile floor, sound asleep in his own vomit. He pulled her up the stairs and along the grungy hallway to Rosia's apartment. He slammed her against the wall and leaned all of his weight into her chest while he took the key from his pocket and unlocked the door.

Inside, the smell of decay and death rushed out to meet them.

"Someone died here." Her voice was shaky; she tried to yank away from him. He punched her in the mouth and she cried out. He watched in fascination as blood flowed from her split lip.

* * *

Gina wanted to run, at least try to run. But she had little strength left, and she knew he wouldn't think twice about killing her on the spot. A she shoved her down a hallway, a horrible stink got stronger and stronger to the point where she was gagging..

On the threshold of the bedroom ,she dug her heels into the threadbare carpet and held on to the door jambs, refusing to take another step. Without a word, he shoved the stiletto into her ass again, deeper this time —the pain shot straight up to top of her head. She screamed, screamed again and rammed an elbow into his chest.

He spun her around and slapped her hard across the face. She started to fall, but he caught her and flung her onto the bed next to a dead woman. The odor of death, mixed with the stink of her own fear, was making her light-headed.

Maria Benke and her mother had been tied down spread-eagle, like this woman. Globs of blood were clotted all over her head and body where he had sliced her. The woman's eyes stared vacantly at the ceiling, her mouth hung open in an expression of terror.

* * *

Pepper Yee looked at the security screen with Tom, who headed Ridgewood's security team.

She wasn't impressed.

Tom was at least fifty pounds overweight and even with that heft, she knew he wouldn't be able to take down a skinny-ass kid, much less anyone who could be real trouble. Even though he was the head honcho at Ridgewood, she would bet his salary probably didn't even equal that of a rookie cop. So why would Tom, or any of the other hire-a-cop, risk their lives no matter what the situation?

"How many of your staff are on duty in the hospital right now?"

"We have a regular force of fifteen, but almost half of them are out sick."

276

A regular fucking army and I'll bet my last dollar they're all just as buff as you.

"Did you check through the tapes?" Pepper asked?

"No, I thought I'd leave that to you."

Of course.

"Okay, let's get to it."

* * *

Harry had been wandering the halls of the hospital, stopping and talking to staff members he knew. The conversations weren't about anything special, he just couldn't go home to their empty apartment.

His insides felt raw and he was scared to death for Gina. He finally gave in and made his way back to Mulzini's room. Harry knew the inspector needed his rest, but he was the only one Harry could really talk to about Gina and the entire situation.

He peeked into Mulzini's room, which was dimly lit. Marcia and Dirk were gone and Mulzini was asleep. He sat down in the chair next to the bed and tried to empty his mind, but he kept coming back to Gina—she'd been taken and she might be a murder victim at this very moment.

"You ought to go home, Harry."

"I thought you were sleeping."

"You ought to go home, " Mulzini repeated.

"Yeah, I know. But I can't. Not yet. I'd feel like I was giving up if I left now ... left before I knew anything certain about Gina.." He looked away, his chest so tight he could barely breathe. "How will I go on without her?"

Mulzini swung his legs around and pushed himself into a sitting position. He leaned toward Harry. "Pepper's good people. She'll find your Gina."

"Yeah, I suppose ... sooner or later."

The inspector reached over and squeezed Harry's shoulder.

Harry snuffed back a sigh, but it didn't stop the tears from flooding his face.

"But will Yee be in time?"

Chapter 60

Pepper Yee had zipped through the elevator security tapes until she was down to the last hour.

"Are all your cameras active?"

"What do you mean, Inspector?"

"You know damn well what I mean. How many are props to fool the public into thinking you have tight security in this *very* public building?"

Tom shifted in his seat, looked away from her. "About half are active."

"Son-of-a-bitch!" Just when she was ready to ream him a new one, she saw Gina in the elevator. She was smiling almost purposely for the camera.

This isn't Hollywood, girl.

She slowed down the streaming and studied the four people in the elevator with Gina, who was in a back corner. When the car stopped, four of the passengers moved like single unit and were out in the snap. Gina followed them out, then turned and went a different direction.

"Okay, Tom,. do you have any surveillance right outside this elevator?"

"Yes, we have two active cameras in that section."

"Well, don't just sit there like a lump. Get me one or both of them on the same time line as that single woman stepping out into the garage to the right."

Tom worked at the computer and had it zipping through time.

"There! Stop!"

A man was carrying Gina over his shoulder. He took her to the back of a Chrysler 300, opened the trunk, and dumped her inside. Once the trunk lid came back down, Yee could read the license plate number. She wrote it down and watched the sedan drive away toward the exit.

"Tom, do you have an active camera at the garage exit?" She held her breath as he fast-forwarded through the tape.

"This might give you what you want."

"I sure as hell hope so."

* * *

Mulzini was worn out; it had been hard watching Harry become so unglued. The man was usually pretty calm and with it. Right now he was looking off through the window, not saying a word. Mulzini could imagine what he was thinking.

The Inspector was starting to doze when the door crashed open and Pepper Yee rushed into the room. A nurse was with her, trying to get her to leave.

"You're not family. You can't go in there." The nurse was annoyed and wasn't giving up on her efforts to keep Yee out of the room, badge or no badge.

Harry turned away from the window, walked up to the nurse, and whispered in her ear. She nodded, gave him a glare, turned around, and went back out the door.

"Hello, Inspector," Harry said in a not-so-nice voice. "Nice to see you again."

"Okay, Harry. I know I blew you off, and I shouldn't have. I apologize."

Before he could respond, she stepped past him to speak to Mulzini. "We've got a BOLO out on the car that took Gina Mazzio away. We grabbed a break with the surveillance cameras ... got the make, model, and license number of the vehicle. Didn't get a clear look at the perp, though."

Mulzini could see Harry taking in every word. He was chalk white.

"Are you heading out?" Mulzini asked.

"Well, yeah!" Yee said, giving him the eye.

"Take Harry with you."

"Are you nuts, Mulzini? You want to put him under fire, too? No way."

"Trust me. He won't be a problem ... will you, Harry?"

Harry shook his head negatively, started toward the door. "All I want is to find Gina." He turned to Yee. "Come on, Inspector, you owe me this one."

She gave Harry a I'd-like-to-strangle-you look and turned to glower at Mulzini. "Oh, man, if this goes south, are you ever gonna get it ... hospital bed or no hospital bed."

"And you!" She pointed at Harry. "No lip! When I say jump, you jump; don't even take time to say, 'How high.'"

Chapter 61

Gina watched the man grab the dead woman by the hair and pull her off the bed, leaving behind a bloody outline of her body. The smell of rot was so strong, she started gagging when acid seared her throat.

"You're a nurse. You've never seen a dead woman before?"

"I've never seen anybody mutilated."

"I am an artist, after all."

"You. You, what's your name? You did this while she was still alive?"

Gina didn't want to die, she would gouge his eyes, kick him in the balls, do anything to get away.

He threw his head back and roared with laughter. "My apologies for not introducing myself. My name is Vlad, Vlad Folo. And your name is Gina Mazzio. He laughed again. "Is that better, Gina Mazzio, the nurse who doesn't like the sight of blood?"

"And you're Vlad Folo, sadistic killer!"

He considered that for a moment. "No, Nurse Mazzio, I'm a businessman. I sell a service and I get no complaints about my work."

Gina scooted away from the bloody outline. "Why would you do that to anyone? Is that what Mort Tallent paid you to do?"

"So you know the good doctor hired me?" He started pulling off his shirt. "Yes, Tallent pays me to kill—and I kill—my way."

Vlad pulled a knife from his pocket and cut away the bottom corners of the bloody sheet, then ripped off four bed-width strips.

"Move to the center of the bed, Nurse Mazzio."

Gina looked into his dead eyes. "I'm not moving into that bloody mess."

He raised the knife high and plunged it deep into her thigh, twisted it before pulling the blade out slowly. He raised it to strike again.

She screamed, "Don't!"

"Move!"

Gina closed her eyes and shifted until she was in the middle of the bed—her blood dripped onto the clotted mess already there.

Vlad took one of the strips of sheet, grabbed her arm, and tied the wrist to the bed post. She struck out at him with her other fist, but he stood by the bed and laughed at her useless jabs.

Gina's heart was thrumming in her ears.

Harry, Harry, I'm going to die.

He jumped on the bed, straddled her, and restrained the other arm. When he finished securing the second wrist, he jumped off the bed, avoiding her thrashing legs.

When he reached for her ankle, she tried to kick him in the face. He stood back and laughed again and suddenly reached out and grabbed her. He muscled-down each leg until she was spread-eagle like his other victims had been.

His smile turned into a leer as he stood in front of her and stripped off the rest of his clothes, then pranced around the bed, turning this way and that to show her his body. He picked up his knife again and methodically cut away her clothes.

"Oops!" he said each time he nicked her skin.

* * *

Harry could see Pepper Yee's adrenalin was high as she drove like a demon shot out of hell. He kept his mouth shut and thought about Gina in the hands of Tallent's mad killer. Yee couldn't drive fast enough for him.

"Listen, Harry, when we get there, don't be a wise ass. I want you to stay in the car ... don't need you to get dusted, too."

Harry turned and looked at her. "You think Gina's dead, don't you?"

"Sorry, Harry. Better to face that possibility now."

"And you think I don't know that?"

"Yeah, well—"

"—who do you think helps put cops together when they come in torn apart, barely hanging on, wanting desperately to live? Who holds their hands when they call out for their women, their men?"

He wanted to crawl inside of Pepper's skin, make her understand there was nothing she could add about life and death or suffering that he didn't already know. But the bottom line— he was grateful she agreed to let him come.

Harry's voice was gone. He spoke in a whisper. "Please, Pepper, don't treat me like a fool."

"Harry—"

"—some maniac has the love of my life. I'm so terrified I'm ready to scream. But if you think I'm going to give up and just accept she's dead, you'd better think again."

Chapter 62

A sudden blast of cold air encircled Vlad.

Mamoushka! If you were here, you would have warned me that black days were coming.

Vlad tried to shake off that sudden feeling of doom settling over him as he stood by the bed and looked down, studied the nurse's nude body from head to toe and back again.

He had goose bumps from the iciness in the room. Why didn't she? She had to feel the cold, the end of her life was but minutes away.

Yes, she had to feel frightened, but there was a glint of anger in her eyes; she still craved life. She hadn't given up hope, like his other victims.

Another blast of cold air jolted him.

Mamoushka!

He wanted to ignore these warnings. But he knew already he'd stayed too long. It was way past time to find a new life far from here.

Put on your clothes. Leave right now. Leave the nurse behind.

Leave!

He tried, but he couldn't turn away, couldn't stop looking at the woman. Her naked body was so close.

He bent over her and mouthed her breasts with his wet lips. "You are very beautiful."

"Get off of me, you piece of shit." But her voice had changed.

Now he saw fear as she tried to jerk away.

Yes. That's better.

He ran his hands up and down his hard, naked body, felt the strength in his loins. He threw himself on top of her, slowly rubbed himself against the length of her smooth, soft body.

Yes, her flesh would yield not only to his heat, but to his knife—like cutting through butter. He reached for his blade on the bedside table, saw the blade was bloody, and for a moment was puzzled.

Yes, now he remembered. He'd stabbed her. Even now her wet running blood was on the bed mixing with Rosia's clotted globules. He would have to clean the blade before he could begin the final ritual.

"Don't go away," he said and gave her a sardonic smile. He stood, grabbed the knife, and walked to the other side of the bed.

When he stepped over Rosia's dead body, he looked down at her and a fresh whiff of death rose to his nostrils.

You're nothing but stinking flesh now. That's all that's left of you, you bitch.

But she'd distracted him.

He was compelled to kneel and looked at the deep slices he'd made across her breasts and stomach.

A memory: Twelve-year-old Vlad coming out of his hiding place in the closet. He'd kneeled at his mother's body as he was doing with Rosia.

These were the same cuts his mother had endured. Those and the long slash that started from her lips and ended at her pubis.

Vlad was shaking, frozen to the bone.

He began to cry. Sobs filled his chest and he moaned over Rosia's body. He took her cold hand and held it. Rocked back and forth.

Mamoushka! Mamoushka!

Then he was emptied.

When he looked down at Rosia's body again, he felt nothing.

Vlad moved into the bathroom and washed the knife until the metal was sparkling clean. When he stepped out, a man was pointing a gun at him.

* * *

Pepper Yee smacked a flashing red light on top of the car to help her cut a pathway through traffic. Harry could only hope that the residence listed on the vehicle registration was not just a ruse. If she wasn't at that address, what next?

He mentally crammed his panic into a box and threw it out the window of the speeding car. But he couldn't stop the numbness that had started in his chest and spread.

Gina had been lucky throughout all of the life-threatening situations she'd gotten into, but today, a man hired for the sole purpose of killing her, had snatched her from the hospital garage.

This all started when Lolly came to San Francisco, got a job at Tallent, Cantor & Brichett. Without Lolly, Gina would never have sneaked into Mort Tallent's office and ended up a murderer's target.

Wasted wishes. He had to stay in the now.

Gina, Gina, Gina! Please be there. Please be alive when we get there.

"Hang in there, Harry. We'll be there in five minutes."

For five minutes his life would be hanging by a thread.

Chapter 63

Gina looked at the man, who seemed to have materialized out of nowhere. One minute there was only her and Vlad, the next minute there was this second man, holding a very large pistol. Anger was etched throughout the deep lines in his face.

"You are the son of Nadya and Ivan Antonev," the man announced, looking at Vlad. The man had not once glanced in Gina's direction.

"So?" Vlad said defiantly. "What do you want here?"

"Drop the knife. Carefully!"

Gina could see the man had fiery eyes and was shaking with emotion.

"Who are you?" Vlad stepped back over Rosia's body.

"I am Alexander Yurev. The one who was supposed to kill you twenty years ago." He backed away, out of Vlad's reach.

Gina yanked on one of the strips of cloth that bound her to the bed. She sensed no weakness. It was solid.

"I'm the one who has been a step behind you for the past twenty years, the one who should have killed you when you were a boy, the Antonev boy. But instead, today you are Vlad Folo, the man. All the same to me: Dimitri Antonev, Karl Pushkin, Vlad Folo. Today you will die ... Dimitri Antonev will finally be dead.

Vlad looked shaken. "I can give you money." All his bravado had melted, his voice was weak, faltering. "All you have to do is forget you ever saw me."

"Money?" Alexander spat out the words. "Did you say money?"

"I can give you fifty thousand dollars. Cash. American."

Alexander stared at him, his neck was red, his back rigid.

"I was just a child," Vlad said. "I had nothing to do with my father's decisions. Why do you blame me?"

Alexander's face flushed a bright red. "I blame you for living, for having a life these twenty years. Everything I had—my wife, my children, my home, my country are gone! So tell me, little boy-man, of what good is fifty thousand American dollars to me now?"

"Please," Vlad said bowing his head.

"When you are dead, I will return to Russia"

"Why would you do that?" Vlad demanded. "As you said, there is nothing left there for you." Vlad smirked as though he had found the key to his freedom—simply tap into Alexander's weakness. "Stay, and with fifty thousand dollars, you can make a new and much better life for yourself."

Gina kept tugging at the strip of sheet. Her skin was raw and burning; her leg wound was painful, continued to seep blood. She ignored the pain, kept pulling at her bonds. She knew that if she didn't get free soon, she would die.

Alexander held the gun with a steady hand. "I will reclaim what is mine when I return to Russia. I will kill anyone who tries to keep me from my family. I will destroy anyone who stole what is mine."

Without warning, Vlad jumped for Alexander. The blast from the pistol filled the room. There was a hole in Vlad's forehead when he fell atop Rosia's body and tumbled onto the floor beside her.

Gina's heart was racing, she could barely breathe. She pulled harder and harder, felt her wrist burn from the friction. She didn't stop yanking and twisting her bonds.

* * *

Alexander Yurev lowered the pistol, wavered for a moment, his face paled, and he looked as though he was going to topple over.

"You should have died twenty years ago," Alexander said, looking down at the dead body of Vlad Folo, lying face up at his feet. "Twenty years of my life wasted looking for you."

Gina yanked again, pain shot up her arm. The strip of sheet was beginning to shred. Then she froze, saw Yurev staring at her. She tried to make herself small, shrink into the mattress, and disappear from the room.

He took a couple of deep breaths and shoved the pistol into a holster under his jacket. He bent and picked up Vlad's knife and walked over to the bed. He stared down at her and she knew he was weighing her value.

"Who are you?" Alexander demanded

"Gina Mazzio. Vlad kidnapped me. He was going to kill me."

Gina could see the man was undecided; he looked deep into her eyes.

Please, please don't kill me. Please, please, please!

He examined her naked body, his eyes continuing to evaluate her. He took in every inch of exposed flesh.

He sighed, checked his watch, and leaned over the bed. Using Vlad's knife, he cut away the strips of sheet from her ankles and wrists.

"You are nothing to me," he said without emotion.

He turned from the bed, walked to the door, and left. She soon heard the apartment door slam shut.

Bette Golden Lamb & J. J. Lamb

294

Chapter 64

"That's the building," Pepper yelled. "Man, this is one ugly neighborhood. I don't even like driving through here."

The rain had stopped, but Harry saw a homeless man covered in plastic sleeping next to a line of garbage cans. Harry knew that if the rain hadn't washed down the streets, the aroma of urine and rotten garbage would probably have made the air near unbreathable.

Pepper double-parked directly behind a squad car. "Looks like my backup beat us here." Two uniformed officers got out and stood by their vehicle, waiting.

"You stay here, Harry, until I see what's up."

"No way. I need to go in with you. If Gina's in there. ... well, that's where I'm going." He could see her lips tighten, ready to turn him down. Instead, she said, "Okay, but stay behind me." She pointed a finger at him. "You hear me, man?"

"Got it!"

They walked up to the two cops. "You guys can wait here in case the perp runs out."

"Come on, Inspector," one of them said. "We didn't come here just to stand and look stupid."

"Okay, you guys follow me." She turned to Harry. "You're at the back of the line."

Harry started to object.

"I swear, Harry, I'll fry your ass if I get screwed because of this."

Harry raised his hands in surrender. "Whatever you say, Inspector." He walked to the entrance of the rundown apartment house, but all he could do was try to shut down an image of Gina's dead body.

Inside the entryway, Yee said, "Looks like Mazzio took part of the wall with her." She pointed to the fresh nail gouges cutting through the paint leading up to the second floor.

A man dressed in wrinkled pants was coming down the stairs. He nodded and gave the four of them a wide smile of crooked teeth. When they let him pass, he said, with the hint of an accent, "Good evening officers."

Standing in front of the apartment door, Pepper drew her gun and pounded on the door.

"SFPD. Open up! Now!"

The patrolmen drew their weapons also, then one of them slid past Yee and kicked open the door. The smell of decay smacked them in the face.

"Holy shit!" Yee said. "What the hell!"

The uniforms spread out, quickly checking the kitchen before moving cautiously down the hallway. When they stepped into the bedroom, the first thing Yee and the cops saw were the two bodies sprawled on the floor.

All Harry saw was Gina, crouched in a corner. Alive!

* * *

Gina had been searching the apartment for something to cover herself when she heard the banging on the door and someone moving down the hall.

What if that man Alexander changed his mind and was coming back to kill her?

She closed her eyes.

Every part of her was screaming in pain. Where Vlad had stabbed her in the buttocks hadn't bled much, but it was throbbing—her wounded thigh was on fire.

Maybe he would shoot her through the heart. End it quickly.

When she finally opened her eyes, Pepper Yee and two other cops were in the room.

And so was Harry.

He ran to her and lifted her up into his arms.

She kissed him on the neck and whispered in his ear, "Don't ask me how, but deep inside, I knew you would come."

"How could you know that, doll?" He'd leaned back and was gently fingering her split lip.

"Because you always do."

Chapter 65

Gina found enough of Rosia's clothes to cover up. She pleaded with Yee not to call the EMTs, and Harry promised the inspector that he would take good care of Gina, make sure she got the proper medical help.

"I really don't get why Mulzini loves you two," Yee said, with a sour look. "If you ask me, you're both pains in the ass."

"We probable are," Harry said. "And I really want to thank you for saving Gina. I'll never forget this, Pepper."

She actually blushed and looked away.

Before they left the apartment, Pepper rested a hand on Harry's arm. "Don't take me too seriously, you know? You're a good man." Then she turned to Gina. "You're lucky to have him."

"Don't I know it."

Gina leaned heavily on Harry as she limped down the apartment building steps and into the back of the squad car.

"Take me home," Gina said, squeezing Harry's hand. "You can steri-strip the wound. I don't want to go to the hospital."

"No way, doll."

Harry asked the cops to take them straight to the Ridgewood ER."

* * *

Gina's thigh needed some heavy duty suturing. The knife had really made a mess of her muscle.

"Steri-strips, huh" Harry whispered in her ear. She smiled, kissed his hand, and held it to her cheek.

She was grateful just to lay back and rest while the ER doc and nurses took care of her. She knew most of them by name; they not only fussed over her serious wound, there were a lot of comments and home remedies for her black eye and split lip.

By the time Harry got her home and into bed, she was pretty much out of it. The last thing she remembered was him saying, "Sleep tight, doll. I'll be right here."

* * *

The next day, Gina spent most of her time sleeping. She'd tried to convince Harry to go to work, but he'd refused. He told her the ICU team leader gave him hell for not coming in, but he stood his ground and promised he'd make it up.

Late in the day, the doorbell rang and Harry opened the door to Vinnie and Helen.

"Thought maybe you and Gina might want to go out and grab a bite for dinner," Vinnie said.

"Nice thought," Harry said, "but not tonight."

"Who's out there?" Gina called from the bedroom.

"Your brother. Was looking forward to your company for dinner. What say?"

"Come on back," Gina yelled.

"Maybe we could do this another night," Harry said.

"Really? What's with you, Harry?" Helen said. She grabbed Vinnie's hand and tugged him toward the bedroom. They stopped in their tracks when they saw Gina in bed.

"What the hell happened to you?" Vinnie said, his voice filled with suspicion. He turned to Harry with questioning eyes.

Harry held up his hands. "Don't look at me that way. You know I would never hurt your sister."

"Maybe not, man, but what happened?"

Helen sat down next to Gina on the edge of the bed. "You look like you've been to the wars."

"It's nothing. I was just sleep-walking, plowed straight into the bathroom door." She laughed. "It about knocked me out."

The phone rang and Harry snatched it up.

"Oh, hi, Mulzini. How you doing?"

He lowered his voice and carried the phone into the kitchen. "She's fine. But it was close."

"Taking care of the two of you is getting to be a full time job," Mulzini said.

"I can't thank you enough for convincing Pepper Yee to get involved right away. The next morning might have been too late."

"Well, I'm glad things worked out. Can't let anything happen to my favorite nurse. Pepper said there was a shooter who killed that Vlad guy who snatched Gina."

"We have to go to the station tomorrow so Gina can give her statement, but it's a real bizarre back story."

"What else can I expect from that crazy nurse of yours?"

"Thanks for calling, Mulzini. But really, how are *you* doing?"

"Hey, I'm fine and it's behind me now."

"We'll be up to see you tomorrow after we give our statements," Harry said. "Again, we really appreciate everything you did."

When Harry turned to go back to the bedroom, Vinnie was standing in the doorway. From the look on his face, Harry knew he'd heard everything."

"Okay, Harry. Out with it! What *really* happened to my sister?"

"Nothing you need to worry about ... now," Harry said.

Vinnie's face flushed and his eyes went cold. "Stop treating me like a damn invalid. Just because I have PTSD doesn't mean you have to shelter me from the world. She's my sister and I have a right to know what's going on with her."

Harry pointed to the dining room table chairs, they sat down next to each other. Harry told Vinnie everything. When he finished, he wrapped an arm around Vinnie's shoulder. "She's okay, man."

Tears ran down Vinnie's cheeks. "I don't understand how so many life-threatening things happen to my sister—anything that can go wrong, always does. It scares the shit out of me."

"Yeah, me too, Vinnie. Me, too." He took a deep breath. "You know, it's not like Gina asks for trouble. Most of the time, like with Tallent, trouble comes to her and she gets sucked into something that should never have involved her in the first place. Know what I mean?"

"Unfortunately, yes."

They went back into the bedroom, where Vinnie gave Gina his usual lecture about her working harder to avoid trouble, then hugged her a long time before letting her go.

* * *

When Helen and Vinnie were gone, Harry locked the door and went back to Gina. He took her in his arms and said, "What am I going to do about you, doll? I'm not sure my heart can take too much more of this, to say nothing about how your antics affect Vinnie."

"It's been hard, I know," she said, looking into his eyes for a long moment.

"I feel so helpless, so lost without you. There must be something I can do to stop the world from crashing down on you."

She took his face in both hands, looked deeply into his eyes.

"Just love me, Harry. That's all I need. Just love me."

-The End-

About the Authors

Bette Golden Lamb & & J. J. Lamb have co-authored a dozen crime novels, plus a few other individual fiction titles as both short stories and books.

Bette is also an RN, with parallel careers as a professional and award-winning painter, sculptor, and ceramist.

J. J. has spent his entire career behind a keyboard as a journalist, freelance writer, editor, and fiction writer, plus, when the occasion demands, he is a competent jack-of-all-trades.

The Lambs have lived in Virginia, New Mexico, New York, Nevada, and currently make their home in Northern California. If you see them at a writers' conference, say *Hello!*

www.twoblacksheep.us